Family Cybersecurity

A Practical Guide to Protecting Your Digital Life

Richard Lowe

The Writing King

Family Cybersecurity: A Practical Guide to Protecting Your Digital Life

Copyright © 2026 by Richard G Lowe

Table of Contents

See books by Richard Lowe at

https://masterofworlds.com

Get free publishing insights and industry updates at

https://thewritingking.substack.com

For ghostwriting and book coaching services see

https://thewritingking.com

Disclaimer

The information provided in this book is for educational purposes only and is based on the author's professional experience and current cybersecurity best practices as of the publication date. Technology and security threats evolve rapidly, and some specific recommendations may become outdated as new vulnerabilities are discovered or as manufacturers change their products and services.

While every effort has been made to provide accurate and practical security guidance, no security system is foolproof, and following the recommendations in this book does not guarantee complete protection against all cyber threats. Readers should supplement this guidance with current threat intelligence and may need to consult with cybersecurity professionals for their specific circumstances.

The author and publisher disclaim any liability for damages resulting from the use or misuse of information contained in this book. Product recommendations are based on features and security capabilities available at the time of writing and do not constitute endorsements or guarantees of these products' continued effectiveness.

Readers are encouraged to verify current security best practices and product capabilities before implementing any recommendations, especially for business or professional use. When in doubt, consult with qualified cybersecurity professionals who can assess your specific situation and requirements.

Forward to the First Edition

Steve Levinson

https://www.linkedin.com/pub/steve-levinson/0/904/217

For over a decade, Richard and I worked together to ensure that Trader Joe's adequately protected credit card data from hackers and criminals. It was a pleasure to work with Richard as he was always extremely conscious of the need for security. He was usually on the same page as me and Jimmy James, the Director of Networking.

Each year my team and I performed Trader Joe's PCI (payment card industry) assessment, which was basically an audit of the security controls pertaining to protecting their credit card data. As Managing Director of OBS Global's security consulting practice, and formerly PCI Practice Director for AT&T Consulting, I've performed hundreds of security assessments/audits. In addition to assessing 'current state of being', I've worked closely with our clients to help ensure that they've created a solid sustainable security program. Richard always had a clear understanding that security is an entity into itself and that it requires constant due diligence and proper care and feeding. Our consulting philosophy is to get to know our customers and their businesses very well so we are in a position to not only measure their security, but to also provide meaningful advice.

During my ten years of having worked with Richard, he had mentioned that he had a dream of becoming a writer, and one of the first books on his list was about home computer security. During those long hours of working together on the audits, we had many conversations about security philosophy and various approaches.

I was happy when Richard informed me he had written this book, and honored when he asked me to review and write a forward. It seemed to align quite nicely with his knowledge, wisdom, and experience. After reviewing the book, I can see that Richard has put in a lot of hard work and effort into the work. His list of best practices are spot on, and those of you who embrace these practices will undoubtedly improve your security posture.

This book will prove to be useful and informative to anyone who uses a computer, especially if you don't know much about computer security. It is written in a manner that is understandable and digestible, which is a welcome treat for those of you who have ever been subjected to trying to read through technical books.

Jimmy James

https://www.linkedin.com/pub/jimmy-james/10/721/a97

While I served as the Director of Networking and Information Security at Trader Joe's, Richard was always talking about writing a book to help the home computer users keep their computer secure. I could see that he was passionate about the subject and believed that he could help home users secure their system, but the book never seemed to get off the ground. The fact of the matter was that we worked for a very large retail chain that had stores all over the country, and this required a lot of our time and energy. Being responsible for managing critical and complex areas of the IT department we were required to work all hours of the day and night, including weekends and holidays.

Richard had a demanding yet very fulfilling position at Trader Joe's, and I could see that he loved being able to contribute to the operation and growth of the company. I could also see that Richard truly believed he could help people with their home computer security and I knew he was sincere about writing a book on the subject. I lost hope that he would be able to finish his book project anytime soon.

When Richard finally retired in October, 2013, he said he was finally going to have time to write the books that he'd been talking about for years. In fact he talked about his dreams and plans for writing and publishing over a dozen books on computers, disaster planning and other interesting subjects. He also had a desire to write a few novels and short stories for publication.

Thus it didn't surprise me at all when Richard called me up and asked me to write a forward for his newest book, *Safe Computing is Like Safe Sex: You have to practice it or you could be infected.*

I enjoyed reading this book. It has a different approach than most other books on home computer security. Other manuscripts I've read focused on technical hacks to the operating system, purchasing equipment, and installing products.

Richard's approach comes from our years of enforcing and practicing sound security at Trader Joe's. We both learned that procedures are far more important than fancy hardware or computer programs.

Thus, I was thrilled to find his focus is to teach home computer users to literally practice safe computing. He lays out a series of best practices which, if followed, will dramatically improve computer security.

I enjoyed reading this book, and to tell you the truth, I will spend some time implementing some of the suggestions on my own home computer.

And finally, Richard, I want you to know that I never doubted that you would complete and publish this book. Now I expect you to get going on all of the other ones you and I talked about and get them done as well. I think you have found your true love.

Ken Cureton

https://www.linkedin.com/in/kencureton

Oh boy. Write a forward for Richard's new book? I'm excited to help! Most folks know him as a photographer, which is just one of his hobbies. I can attest that he's a great writer as well!

Richard and I go way back. I mean way back, to the early 1980s. Further than I like to think about. He was working at a small computer company called Software Techniques and my company, Command Computer Systems Incorporated, had contracted with him to write some custom software to allow our computer programs to access data over a network of computers, something that we take for granted nowadays, but very cutting-edge back then.

In those days, Richard was always serious, overly serious. On the other hand, he had a biting sense of humor, which is one of the reasons we became friends. His humor is well, humorously sarcastic. Really, he's a funny man when he wants to be.

The book is very, very good. If you are a home computer user you need to know the dangers that you face every day you venture out onto the internet. It's a wild place, full of hackers and thieves and trolls... no wait. No trolls. Oh yes, there are trolls, aren't there?

Okay, so I met Richard while I was the Vice President of a computer company called Command Computer Systems Incorporated. I'd better mention how easy he was to work with as well as his fantastic personality... sorry, you said no sarcasm? Oh, sorry. Where was I?

Oh yes, Richard was the Vice President of Consulting at Software Techniques. We did a project together and it went very well. I was impressed because he was thorough, the project was completed on time, and within budget. Oh, and his software actually worked as specified. How often can you say all of that?

Over the years he and I stayed in contact and our friendship grew. I remember when Richard got married, out of the blue, after a two-week courtship. Twelve years later Richard was a widower, having remained with his wife, Claudia, through a ten year chronic illness. Now that's integrity.

Now he's written a book. I know he's passionate about this subject, and he certainly has the experience. He worked for 20 years at Trader Joe's and was one of the people in charge of their computer security. That's a tough position, and I know he did it very well.

Buy this book. Read this book. I recommend it without reservation. The knowledge you gain will help you keep the information on your computer secure and safe from evildoers. And to all the evildoers out there—beware! Richard is telling everyone all about your secrets. ALL of them!

Preface

The phone rang at 2:47 AM. I knew before I picked it up that someone's digital life had just exploded.

"Richard, I need help. Everything's gone."

My friend's voice cracked as she described watching thirty years of family photos vanish from her computer screen. Wedding pictures. Baby's first steps. Her mother's last Christmas before cancer took her. All of it disappeared because she clicked one innocent-looking email attachment.

I threw on clothes and drove to her house, carrying every data recovery tool I owned. We worked until dawn, trying everything I'd learned in thirty-five years of computer security. Nothing worked. The ransomware had encrypted every precious memory on her hard drive, and the criminals wanted \$500 to maybe give them back.

She paid. They kept the money and the photos.

That morning changed how I think about computer security. All those years protecting corporate networks and million-dollar systems, I'd forgotten something crucial: the most devastating attacks don't target banks or governments. They target ordinary families who store their entire lives on devices they barely understand.

Your smartphone holds more personal information than any government file ever compiled on you. Your laptop contains financial records that could bankrupt you if stolen. Your smart doorbell records who visits your home. Your children's tablets know their schedules, their friends, their fears. Every device in your house connects to the internet, and every connection creates an opportunity for someone with bad intentions.

The criminals have evolved. Twenty years ago, hackers were mostly curious teenagers showing off to their friends. Today, cybercrime generates more revenue than the global drug trade. Professional crime organizations employ thousands of people whose only job is stealing your information and money. They punch in at 9 AM, take lunch breaks, and go home to their families after spending eight hours figuring out new ways to ruin yours.

They target families because families are easy. You don't have million-dollar security budgets or teams of IT professionals. You have kids who click on everything, teenagers who share passwords, and grandparents who believe every email that claims to be from their bank. You have smart speakers listening to your conversations, security cameras that strangers can access, and tablets that remember every website anyone in your household has ever visited.

Most security books read like technical manuals written by engineers for engineers. They assume you want to become a cybersecurity expert instead of just protecting your family's digital life. They drown you in jargon, overwhelm you with complicated procedures, and leave you more confused than when you started.

This book takes a different approach. Every technique I recommend, I use on my own devices. Every story I tell happened to real people I know. Every chapter starts with someone learning an expensive lesson, so you don't have to.

You'll learn how criminals see your home network, what they want from your devices, and exactly how to stop them. More importantly, you'll understand why certain security measures matter and others are just security theater. I'll show you how to protect your family without turning your home into a fortress or driving everyone crazy with complicated rules.

> ★ **Pro Tip:** Security that's too hard to use gets ignored. The best protection is the kind that works automatically in the background while you live your life.

The techniques in this book don't require technical expertise or expensive equipment. They assume you have better things to do than become a computer security expert. You want to check email, share photos with family, let your kids play games online, and shop for groceries without worrying that criminals are watching every click.

Some security advice sounds paranoid because it is paranoid. I won't tell you to disconnect from the internet or throw your smartphones in a drawer. Technology should make your life better, not more stressful. The goal is reasonable protection against realistic threats, not perfect security against imaginary attackers.

After three decades of cleaning up security disasters, I've learned that most attacks succeed not because the technology failed, but because someone made a simple mistake. They used their birthday as a password. They clicked a link without thinking. They assumed their home network was automatically secure. They never made a backup until it was too late.

> ▲ **Caution:** The most dangerous phrase in computer security is "that would never happen to me." Criminals count on that attitude.

Your family's digital safety doesn't require perfection. You need good habits, basic protection, and the knowledge to recognize when something's wrong. You need to understand how your devices work together and what happens when one gets compromised. Most importantly, you need a plan for when things go bad, because eventually something will go wrong.

The stories in this book come from real security incidents involving real families. I've changed names and details to protect privacy, but every disaster happened. The friend who lost her photos. The coworker who paid ransom but got nothing back. The neighbor whose unsecured wireless network got him investigated by the FBI. The grandmother whose predictable password cost her life savings.

These people weren't stupid or careless. They just didn't know what they didn't know. They learned about digital security the same way most of us learn about home security: after someone breaks in.

You don't have to learn the hard way. This book contains thirty-five years of experience protecting computer systems, distilled into practical advice for protecting what matters most to you. Your family's photos. Your financial information. Your children's safety. Your peace of mind.

The criminals are counting on you to stay confused and vulnerable. Let's prove them wrong.

Introduction: Why Every Family Needs This Book

I heard a horrible screech from the drive and knew everything was gone.

The sound came from my external hard drive at three on a Tuesday afternoon. I was editing a photo from my latest shoot when the drive made a noise like fingernails on a chalkboard, then went silent. Thirty years of photography. Three hundred thousand images. Weddings, portraits, national parks, Renaissance festivals. Gone.

That drive contained my entire professional portfolio. I'd been meaning to make a backup "tomorrow" for months. Tomorrow became next week, next week became next month, and next month became the day I learned why everyone in computer security obsesses about backups.

I spent the next three weeks nursing that dying drive back to life ten minutes at a time, copying files before it overheated and shut down again. I recovered most of them, but barely.

This disaster taught me something crucial: knowing about computer security professionally doesn't automatically protect your personal life. I'd spent decades securing corporate networks worth millions of dollars, but I couldn't be bothered to back up my own irreplaceable photos. Classic case of the cobbler's children having no shoes.

Your family faces the same gap between knowing what you should do and doing it. You understand that passwords matter, but you still use your pet's name because it's easier to remember. You know you should update your software, but you keep clicking "remind me later" because you're busy. You realize backing up files makes sense, but you'll get around to it eventually.

Criminals exploit this gap. They count on you knowing the right thing to do but not actually doing it. They design attacks around human nature: our tendency to procrastinate, our desire for convenience, our willingness to trust people who seem helpful.

◆ **Personal Experience:** The biggest security breach I ever witnessed happened because someone propped open a locked door with a brick. The company had spent thousands on card readers, security cameras, and alarm systems. None of it mattered when an employee got tired of digging out his badge every time he stepped outside for a smoke break.

Your home network faces similar challenges. You can install the best security software money can buy, but it won't help if your teenager downloads infected games or your spouse clicks every link that promises free gift cards. Family cybersecurity succeeds or fails based on the habits of your weakest link.

Most security books focus on technology instead of people. They assume you want to become a cybersecurity expert rather than just protect your family. They overwhelm you with technical details about firewalls, encryption protocols, and network monitoring tools that most families will never need.

This book focuses on the human side of security. You'll learn why certain attacks work, how criminals choose their targets, and what you can do to make your family less appealing prey. You'll discover that protecting your digital life has more to do with good habits than good software.

★ **Pro Tip:** Security that depends on perfect behavior from every family member will fail. Build systems that work even when people make mistakes.

Every chapter starts with a real story about real people learning expensive lessons. The friend who lost twenty years of family photos to ransomware. The coworker whose birthday password cost him his life savings. The neighbor whose unsecured wireless network attracted FBI attention. The grandmother whose "helpful" phone call gave criminals access to her bank account.

These people weren't careless or stupid. They just didn't know what they didn't know. They assumed their antivirus software would catch everything. They thought criminals only targeted big companies. They believed their small-town location made them safe from cyber attacks.

Wrong on all counts.

Cybercrime is now a larger industry than illegal drug trafficking. Professional criminal organizations employ thousands of people whose job is stealing your money and information. They use sophisticated tools, proven techniques, and industrial-scale operations to separate families from their digital assets.

They target regular households because you're easier prey than corporations. You don't have security teams monitoring your network traffic. You don't have policies governing password use. You don't have backup systems and recovery procedures. You just have busy lives and devices you barely understand.

> ▲ **Caution:** Criminals don't take weekends off. Your home network needs protection 24/7, even when you're sleeping.

The attacks keep evolving. Email scams that used to contain obvious spelling errors now look identical to legitimate messages from your bank. Fake websites that once screamed "scam" now perfectly mimic real company pages. Phone calls from "tech support" sound increasingly professional and convincing.

Meanwhile, your attack surface keeps growing. Smart speakers listen to your conversations. Security cameras record your daily routines. Fitness trackers monitor your health. Cars report your driving habits. Every new device creates fresh opportunities for criminals to access your personal information.

You can't eliminate every risk, but you can manage the ones that matter most. You can make your family a harder target than your neighbors. You can create systems that protect you even when individual devices get compromised. You can prepare for attacks so you recover quickly instead of losing everything.

> ■ **Danger Zone:** The phrase "I have nothing to hide" is code for "I don't understand what I'm risking." Everyone has something worth protecting, even if it's just family photos and financial records.

This book teaches practical protection, not paranoid perfection. You'll learn which threats are real and which are overblown. You'll discover security measures that work versus security theater that just makes you feel safer. You'll understand when to spend money on protection and when good habits provide better defense.

The goal is reasonable security for normal families. You want to check email, share photos, shop online, and let your kids use the internet without constant worry about digital disasters. You want protection that works automatically in the background while you live your life.

That protection starts with understanding how criminals see your home network and what they want from your devices. Time to learn how the game really works.

Part I: Understanding Your Digital Home

Chapter 1: Your Connected Home - The New Reality

My neighbor's baby monitor broadcasted to the entire neighborhood

---

The Kowalskis discovered their privacy problem when Mrs. Patel from across the street knocked on their door at 7 AM. "I can hear your baby crying through my kitchen radio," she said, holding up an old transistor radio crackling with the sound of little Emma's morning fussing.

Their baby monitor was broadcasting on the same frequency as AM radio. Every conversation in Emma's room, every bedtime story, every private moment between parents and child was transmitting to anyone within a quarter-mile who happened to tune to 1680 on the AM dial.

The Kowalskis thought they'd bought a simple baby monitor. They brought home a radio transmitter with no security, no password, and no privacy. For six months, their neighbors had accidentally eavesdropped on their most intimate family moments.

The baby monitor wasn't broken. It worked exactly as designed. The Kowalskis just didn't understand what they'd purchased: a device that connected their private space to the outside world.

Your home probably contains dozens of devices that do the same thing. Each one was designed to make your life more convenient, but together they've turned your house into something new: a connected home where your private space constantly communicates with the outside world.

Your House Is Now a Computer Network

Your home's internet connection works like the main water pipe that brings water into your house. That pipe connects to smaller pipes that carry water to every faucet, toilet, and appliance. Your internet connection branches out the same way to reach every device in your home that needs to get online.

This branching system is called a network. The box your internet company installed (they might call it a modem, router, or gateway) acts like the main junction where your internet connection splits to reach all your devices. Some devices connect with wires, but most connect wirelessly through invisible radio signals.

Every device that connects to your network can potentially talk to every other device. Your laptop sends files to your printer. Your phone controls your smart TV. Your tablet accesses photos stored on your desktop computer. This interconnection makes your devices more useful, but problems spread quickly from one device to another.

When people talk about "home networks" or "wireless networks," they're describing this system of connected devices in your house. You don't need to understand how it works technically, but you do need to understand that it exists and what it means for your family's privacy and safety.

Counting Your Connected Life

Walk through your house and count the devices that connect to your internet. Start in the kitchen: smart refrigerator, microwave with WiFi, voice assistant, coffee maker you can start from your phone. Move to the living room: smart TV, streaming devices, gaming consoles, sound system, smart speakers.

Don't forget the less obvious ones. Security system panels, thermostats, light switches, door locks, garage door openers. Your car in the driveway probably connects to your home WiFi to download updates. Even washing machines and dryers now connect to the internet.

In bedrooms, count phones, tablets, laptops, smart watches, fitness trackers, e-readers, alarm clocks that sync with your phone. Kids' rooms often have gaming devices, educational tablets, and smart toys that connect online.

Most families have between 25 and 60 connected devices without realizing it. Each device contains a computer more powerful than the systems that ran entire corporations thirty years ago. Each stores information about your habits, preferences, and daily routines. Each talks to servers controlled by companies you've probably never heard of.

Your connected devices constantly share information with each other and with companies outside your home. Your smart TV reports what shows you watch. Your fitness tracker uploads your exercise data. Your smart speaker sends recordings to servers for voice processing. Your phone's apps share your location with advertisers.

Most of this data sharing happens automatically in the background. You don't see it, you don't control it, and you probably didn't agree to most of it. The agreements are buried in legal documents that take hours to read and understand.

Real Consequences for Real Families

When Smart TVs Turn Against You

The Brennan family learned about smart TV vulnerabilities when criminals took control of their television for three months. The TV's microphone had been activated remotely, recording conversations about their work schedules, vacation plans, and financial problems. The criminals never gained access to a camera because their TV didn't have one, but the microphone was enough.

Criminals used this information to plan a burglary during the family's ski trip. They knew exactly when the house would be empty, what valuables to look for, and even where spare keys were hidden based on overheard conversations. The theft wasn't random. It was orchestrated using intelligence gathered through their own smart TV's microphone.

The TV never showed any signs of compromise. It played Netflix normally, responded to the remote, and displayed perfect picture quality. The family had no idea they were being listened to until police investigating the burglary discovered the spy software during a forensic examination.

This attack happened through a vulnerability in the TV's streaming software. Criminals had compromised a popular streaming app and used it to install listening software on thousands of TVs. The malware was designed to record conversations when it detected certain keywords like "vacation," "bank," or "password." The recordings were automatically uploaded to criminal servers and analyzed for useful information.

The Brennan family's TV had been infected for months before the burglary. During that time, criminals learned the family's daily routines, financial discussions, and travel plans. They even knew which rooms contained the most valuable electronics because family members had discussed insurance valuations within range of the TV's microphone.

The attack was discovered only because the burglars made a mistake. They used information that could only have come from inside the house, which led police to examine the family's connected devices. The forensic investigation revealed that the TV had been sending audio files to servers in Eastern Europe for months.

Children's Devices Create Family Risks

Twelve-year-old Ashley loved her new fitness tracker until it led criminals to her family's front door. The device's GPS function shared her location data with a fitness app, which sold that information to data brokers, who combined it with other sources to build a detailed profile of the family's daily routines.

Criminals purchased this profile data for $3 and used it to plan identity theft. They knew when Ashley walked to school (8:15 AM), when her mother left for work (8:45 AM), and when the house sat empty (9 AM to 3:30 PM weekdays). They used this window to steal mail containing pre-approved credit card offers and tax documents.

The family discovered the identity theft six months later when they applied for a car loan and learned their credit had been destroyed. Ashley's innocent desire to track her daily steps had created a data trail that led criminals directly to her family's financial information.

Smart Home Devices Become Burglary Tools

The Volkov family's smart doorbell was supposed to make them safer. Instead, it helped criminals plan the perfect break-in. The doorbell's default password had never been changed, and criminals gained access to its cloud storage account where video footage was stored.

Criminals monitored the camera feeds for weeks, learning the family's patterns. They discovered that packages were delivered at 2 PM on Tuesdays and Thursdays, when nobody was home. They watched the family hide a spare key under a fake rock by the front steps. They even observed which rooms contained the most valuable electronics.

The burglary happened on a Thursday afternoon. Criminals disabled the doorbell's internet connection, used the hidden key to enter, and stole $15,000 worth of electronics and jewelry. They were in and out in twelve minutes, knowing exactly what to take and where to find it because they'd been watching the family for a month.

How Family Members Create Different Risks

Teenagers: The Weak Link You Love

Your teenagers create the biggest security risks in your home, often without realizing it. They download games from sketchy websites, share passwords with friends, and click on links that promise free music or movie downloads. Their devices often have access to family photos, shared cloud storage, and the same network as your financial computers.

Sixteen-year-old Marcus thought he was downloading a harmless game modification. The file contained malware that spread from his gaming computer to the family's shared photo storage, then to his parents' laptops when they synced family pictures. The malware recorded passwords, copied tax documents, and gave criminals access to three bank accounts.

The attack succeeded because Marcus's gaming computer could reach the same network resources as his parents' devices. His casual approach to internet security became everyone's problem when malware used his computer as a launching pad to attack the rest of the family's devices.

⚠ **Caution:** Teenagers often resist security restrictions because they see them as "paranoid parent stuff." Frame security as protecting their own privacy and future opportunities, not just family safety.

Children: Innocents Who Share Everything

Young children create risks by oversharing personal information online. They post photos that reveal your home address, share family vacation plans on social media, and accept friend requests from strangers who seem friendly. They don't understand that information shared online stays online forever.

Eight-year-old Sophie loved showing off her art projects on a kids' social media platform. She innocently included photos of her bedroom, which showed family photos containing her parents' full names on the walls. She posted pictures of her school uniform, identifying where she attended classes. She shared excitement about the family's upcoming Disney World trip, including dates and hotel information.

Criminals used this information to attempt identity theft, create fake social media profiles pretending to be family friends, and even called the school pretending to be relatives authorized to pick up Sophie. The family's innocent desire to encourage their daughter's creativity had exposed them to multiple threats.

Grandparents: Trusting Targets

Elderly family members often fall for social engineering attacks because they trust people who claim to be helpful. They receive phone calls from "tech support" offering to fix computer problems, emails from "banks" asking them to verify account information, and messages from "grandchildren" asking for emergency money.

Grandpa Joe received a call from someone claiming to be from his computer company's technical support department. The caller knew his name, address, and what type of computer he owned (information purchased from data brokers). They convinced him to install remote access software so they could "fix security problems" on his computer.

The criminals used this access to steal passwords, copy financial documents, and install keylogging software that recorded everything Joe typed. They gained access to his online banking, investment accounts, and email. Within a week, they'd stolen $23,000 and used his email account to send scam messages to his entire contact list, including other family members.

The Hidden Web of Connections

How Your Doorbell Talks to Your Bank Account

Modern smart devices share information in ways that create unexpected security vulnerabilities. Your smart doorbell might seem unrelated to your online banking, but here's how they connect:

Your doorbell connects to your home WiFi network using a password. If criminals hack the doorbell, they can extract that password and use it to connect their own devices to your network. Once on your network, they can potentially access any device that uses the same WiFi connection, including your laptop where you do online banking.

The doorbell also uploads video footage to cloud servers controlled by the manufacturer. If those servers get hacked (and many have been), criminals can access footage from thousands of homes simultaneously. They use this footage to identify valuable targets, plan burglaries, and even blackmail families caught in compromising situations.

When Fitness Trackers Reveal Family Secrets

Your family's fitness trackers create a detailed map of your daily routines without you realizing it. The devices track not just your exercise, but your location throughout the day, your sleep patterns, and even your heart rate during stressful situations.

This data gets shared with fitness apps, which sell it to data brokers, who combine it with information from other sources. The result is profiles that reveal when you leave for work, how long you're gone, where you shop, and when you travel. Criminals buy these profiles to plan identity theft and burglaries.

The Okafor family discovered this connection when their house was burglarized during their vacation to Mexico. Criminals had purchased location data showing that all family members' fitness trackers had been stationary at a resort in Cancun for five days. They used this information to confirm the house was empty and plan the break-in.

How Smart TVs Share Your Shopping Habits

Your smart TV doesn't just track what shows you watch. It also monitors the advertisements you see, how long you watch them, and whether you change channels during commercials. This advertising data gets combined with your shopping history, social media activity, and search history to create detailed consumer profiles.

> ▲ **Caution:** Many smart TVs come with microphones that can be remotely activated by hackers. Unlike cameras (which most modern TVs don't have), microphones are common and represent a real privacy risk.

These profiles get sold to companies that use them for targeted advertising, but they also get stolen by criminals who use them for identity theft. Your TV viewing habits reveal your income level, family composition, and personal interests. Combined with data from other sources, this information helps criminals create convincing phishing attacks tailored to your family.

> **★ Pro Tip:** Check your smart TV's privacy settings and turn off as much data collection as possible. Most TVs work fine without sending viewing data to manufacturers. Also disable the microphone when not using voice commands.

What This Means for Daily Family Life

Your Children's Digital Footprints Follow Them Forever

Every photo your children post online, every game they play, every app they download creates a permanent digital record. These records get collected by companies, sold to data brokers, and used to build profiles that could affect your children's future job prospects, insurance rates, and even college admissions.

Colleges and employers routinely search social media profiles during application processes. That embarrassing photo from your teenager's party could cost them a scholarship. That angry comment they posted during a bad day could affect their job prospects years later.

Your Smart Home Devices Create Security Dependencies

When you connect multiple devices to create a smart home environment, you create dependencies that can cascade into major problems. If criminals compromise your smart home hub, they might gain access to door locks, security cameras, and alarm systems all at once.

The Nakamura family learned this when hackers took control of their smart home system and used it to harass them. Criminals turned lights on and off randomly, changed thermostat settings to uncomfortable temperatures, and played loud music through connected speakers at 3 AM. They even unlocked doors and disabled security cameras to prove they had complete control.

The harassment continued for weeks because the criminals had access to the central hub that controlled all connected devices. The family had to replace their entire smart home system and change all their passwords to regain control of their own house.

Your Family's Location Data Is Always Being Tracked

Your family members carry multiple tracking devices everywhere they go. Phones, fitness trackers, smart watches, and even some clothing items now contain GPS chips that record location data constantly. This information gets shared with apps, advertisers, and data brokers without your explicit consent.

Location data reveals personal information about your family's habits, relationships, and activities. It shows where your children go after school, whether your spouse stops anywhere on the way home from work, and how often you visit doctors or other sensitive locations.

> ■ **Danger Zone:** Location data from family devices has been used to plan kidnappings, stalk domestic violence victims, and target families for burglary. Turn off location sharing for all apps that don't absolutely need it.

Your Home Network Reflects Your Family's Vulnerabilities

Every family member's online habits affect the security of your entire home network. Your teenager's risky downloading habits can infect devices used by other family members. Your elderly parent's susceptibility to scams can compromise shared email accounts. Your child's social media oversharing can reveal information about your family's routines and financial status.

The interconnected nature of modern homes means that your family's security is only as strong as its weakest member. You can't just protect individual devices; you need to think about how family members' different risk levels interact with your connected environment.

This reality requires a family-wide approach to digital security. Everyone needs to understand how their actions affect others, and you need systems that protect against mistakes instead of assuming perfect behavior from every family member.

These connections and risks are what you need to grasp before building effective defenses. First, though, you need to know who wants to exploit these vulnerabilities and why your family makes an attractive target.

Chapter 2: Who's Trying to Harm Your Family and Why

Hackers dressed as repair technicians trying to replace our credit card readers

---

The phone call came at 6 AM on a Tuesday. "Sir, this is David from your credit card processing company. We've detected suspicious activity on your merchant account and need to replace your card readers immediately. Our technicians are already in your area and can be there in twenty minutes."

I was barely awake, but something felt wrong. Our retail stores used a different processing company, and they'd never called this early. I stalled the caller while I checked our actual account online. Everything looked normal.

Twenty minutes later, two men in polo shirts with fake company logos knocked on our back door, carrying official-looking equipment cases. They had badges, clipboards, and knew just enough about our business to sound legitimate. But their "replacement" card readers were designed to steal every customer's credit card information.

These weren't random thieves hoping to grab cash from the register. They were professional criminals running an organized operation to harvest credit card data from dozens of businesses. They'd researched our company, created fake credentials, and planned every detail of their con.

The scary part? They almost succeeded. If I hadn't been paranoid enough to verify their story, we might have handed over our customers' financial information to criminals without realizing it.

Your family faces the same level of sophisticated, organized criminal activity every day. The people trying to harm you aren't random hackers working alone in basements. They're part of a global industry that generates more revenue than most Fortune 500 companies.

The Evolution of Digital Crime

Twenty years ago, most computer criminals were curious teenagers showing off to their friends. They wrote viruses for fame, not money. They wanted to prove they could break into systems, not steal your life savings. The worst they usually did was crash your computer or display annoying messages.

Those days are over.

Today's cybercriminals punch time clocks at office buildings in major cities. They have human resources departments, vacation policies, and performance bonuses. They use sophisticated project management software to coordinate attacks across multiple countries. They have customer service departments to help victims pay ransoms more efficiently.

◆ **Personal Experience:** I attended a cybersecurity conference where researchers had infiltrated criminal organizations and recorded their internal communications. These groups operated like any other business, complete with employee handbooks, training programs, and retirement plans. One ransomware group even had a complaints department to handle victims who felt their "customer service" was inadequate.

The transformation happened because digital crime became incredibly profitable. Why rob convenience stores for a few hundred dollars when you can steal millions from the comfort of your home office? Why risk jail time for physical crimes when digital attacks are harder to trace and prosecute?

Cybercrime now generates more revenue than the global drug trade. Conservative estimates put annual cybercrime profits at over $6 trillion globally. That's more money than most countries' entire gross domestic product.

This money attracts serious criminal organizations with serious resources. They hire the best programmers, buy the most advanced tools, and operate with the efficiency of multinational corporations.

Who Wants to Harm Your Family

Organized Crime Syndicates

The biggest threat to your family comes from organized criminal groups that operate like technology companies. These organizations employ hundreds of specialists: programmers who write malware, social engineers who design convincing scams, money launderers who clean stolen funds, and customer service representatives who help victims pay ransoms.

Eastern European crime syndicates dominate the ransomware industry. Groups like REvil, Conti, and DarkSide operate from countries where local governments either can't or won't prosecute them. They recruit talent from top universities, offer competitive salaries, and provide full benefits packages to their employees.

These groups don't target random victims. They research potential targets for weeks or months before attacking. They know how much money you have, what devices you use, and when you're most vulnerable. They tailor their attacks to your specific situation and psychology.

Russian-speaking criminal organizations control most of the world's ransomware operations. They operate under informal agreements with their governments: don't attack domestic targets, and we'll leave you alone. This protection allows them to operate openly, advertising their services on criminal forums and recruiting new members through job postings.

Nation-State Actors

Foreign governments employ thousands of hackers to steal information, disrupt infrastructure, and influence public opinion. These state-sponsored groups have unlimited budgets, advanced tools, and legal immunity in their home countries.

China's Ministry of State Security runs APT (Advanced Persistent Threat) groups that steal intellectual property from American families and businesses. They're not just targeting Fortune 500 companies; they're also interested in innovative small businesses, promising students, and anyone with valuable information or connections.

North Korea funds its nuclear program partly through cybercrime. The Lazarus Group, controlled by North Korean intelligence, has stolen billions of dollars through bank heists, cryptocurrency theft, and ransomware attacks. They target everyone from major financial institutions to individual cryptocurrency investors.

Iran operates sophisticated disinformation campaigns designed to influence American elections and social policies. They create fake social media accounts, spread divisive content, and amplify existing political tensions to destabilize democratic processes.

> ▲ **Caution:** Nation-state attacks on families usually focus on information gathering rather than immediate financial theft. They're building long-term intelligence profiles that might be used years later.

Criminal-as-a-Service Operations

The cybercrime industry has evolved to offer "crime-as-a-service" platforms where anyone can rent criminal tools and services. You don't need technical skills to launch sophisticated attacks anymore; you just need money to rent the necessary tools and expertise.

Ransomware-as-a-Service (RaaS) platforms let amateur criminals rent professional-grade ransomware and support services. The platform provides the malware, handles payment processing, negotiates with victims, and takes a percentage of any ransoms collected. It's like Uber for digital extortion.

Botnet-as-a-Service platforms rent access to networks of infected computers. Criminals can rent 10,000 infected machines for a few hundred dollars and use them to send spam, mine cryptocurrency, or launch denial-of-service attacks.

Phishing-as-a-Service platforms provide everything needed to run convincing email scams: fake websites, stolen email lists, and even customer support to help victims enter their credentials on fraudulent login pages.

These platforms have democratized cybercrime. A teenager with $500 can now launch attacks that were previously limited to sophisticated criminal organizations.

Individual Scammers and Fraudsters

While organized crime gets the headlines, individual scammers and small criminal groups pose the most immediate threat to most families. These criminals use simpler techniques but target more people, playing a numbers game where even a small success rate generates significant profits.

Romance scammers create fake profiles on dating websites and social media platforms to build emotional relationships with lonely victims. They spend months building trust before asking for money to handle "emergencies" or travel expenses to meet in person.

Tech support scammers call random phone numbers claiming to be from Microsoft, Apple, or other major technology companies. They convince victims that their computers are infected and need immediate attention, then charge hundreds of dollars for unnecessary "repairs" while installing real malware.

Social Security scammers call elderly victims claiming their benefits are suspended due to suspicious activity. They demand immediate payment to restore benefits and threaten arrest if victims don't comply.

These scammers succeed because they understand human psychology better than technology. They don't need advanced hacking skills; they just need to sound convincing enough to trick people into voluntarily handing over money or information.

Why Criminals Target Regular Families

You Have More Than You Think

Criminals target regular families because you have more valuable information than you realize. Your home contains devices that store financial records, personal photos, medical information, work documents, and social connections. This combination of information is often more valuable than what criminals can steal from individual businesses.

Your family's data creates a complete picture of your life that criminals can monetize in multiple ways. They can sell your financial information to other criminals, use your personal photos for blackmail, access your work systems through your home devices, and impersonate you to scam your friends and family.

The average American family has access to financial accounts worth tens of thousands of dollars, owns property worth hundreds of thousands of dollars, and maintains relationships with hundreds of people who trust them. Criminals see all of this as potential profit.

Your children's information is particularly valuable because it can be used for long-term identity theft. A criminal who steals a child's Social Security number can use it for decades before the theft is discovered. By the time your child applies for their first credit card or student loan, their identity might already be compromised.

You're Easier Targets Than Businesses

Large corporations spend millions of dollars on cybersecurity and employ teams of security professionals. They have policies, procedures, and technologies designed to detect and respond to attacks quickly.

Your family has none of that protection. You don't have a security team monitoring your network traffic. You don't have policies governing password use or data sharing. You don't have backup systems and incident response procedures. You just have busy lives and devices you barely understand.

Criminals know this disparity and exploit it ruthlessly. Why attack a bank with sophisticated security systems when you can attack thousands of families with no security at all? The individual payoff might be smaller, but the success rate is much higher.

Business networks are also more likely to be monitored by law enforcement and security researchers. Attacks on major corporations make headlines and trigger investigations. Attacks on families often go unnoticed until the damage is already done.

You're Connected to Valuable Targets

Even if your family doesn't seem like an attractive target, you're connected to people and organizations that are. Criminals use attacks on families as stepping stones to reach more valuable targets.

Your work email account, accessible from your home computer, might provide access to your employer's network. Your children's school accounts might lead to educational databases containing thousands of families' information. Your elderly parent's healthcare accounts might provide access to medical systems.

Criminals wanted to steal intellectual property from a defense contractor, but the company's security was too strong for direct attacks. Instead, they targeted the teenage daughter of a senior engineer.

The criminals spent months building a fake romantic relationship with the girl through social media. They convinced her to install a "special messaging app" so they could communicate privately. The app was malware that gave criminals access to her phone.

The girl's phone connected to her family's home WiFi network, which her father also used for work. The father occasionally checked work email from his personal laptop, which shared the same network as his daughter's infected phone.

Criminals used the daughter's phone as a bridge to reach the father's laptop, then used the laptop to access the company's email system. From there, they spent six months slowly stealing product designs and technical specifications worth millions of dollars.

The attack succeeded because criminals understood that the path to their real target ran through a seemingly unrelated family member. The defense contractor never suspected that their security breach started with a fake teenage romance.

Criminals map these connections systematically. They research employees at target companies, identify their family members, and look for the weakest security links. Your elderly parent's poor password habits might be the key to compromising your employer's network.

How They Choose Their Targets

Data Brokers Provide the Intelligence

Criminals don't choose targets randomly. They buy detailed information about potential victims from data brokers, who collect and sell personal information from hundreds of sources.

Data brokers know your income level, shopping habits, family composition, political views, health conditions, and financial status. They sell this information to advertisers, but criminals buy it too. For less than $50, a criminal can purchase detailed profiles of hundreds of families in specific income ranges or geographic areas.

This intelligence gathering goes far beyond what you might expect. Data brokers track your online purchases to estimate your disposable income. They monitor your social media activity to identify your interests and psychological triggers. They correlate your location data with census information to build detailed demographic profiles.

Armed with this information, criminals can craft highly targeted attacks. They know which families are likely to have savings worth stealing, which psychological triggers will make victims more compliant, and which family members are most vulnerable to specific types of scams.

Social Media Provides the Details

Your family's social media activity provides criminals with detailed intelligence about your routines, relationships, and vulnerabilities. You might think your privacy settings protect you, but criminals have ways to access information even from "private" accounts.

Children often have weaker privacy settings than adults and share more personal information. Criminals research children's accounts to learn about family vacations, financial discussions, and daily routines. They piece together information from multiple family members to build complete intelligence pictures.

Geotagged photos reveal your home address, workplace, and frequently visited locations. Check-ins at restaurants and events tell criminals when you're away from home. Photos of expensive purchases or home improvements indicate your income level and what's worth stealing.

Family relationship information helps criminals plan social engineering attacks. They learn the names of family members, friends, and colleagues, then use this information to make scam calls and emails more convincing.

> ★ **Pro Tip:** Criminals often research their targets for months before attacking. Review your family's social media activity as if you were planning to rob yourselves. What would criminals learn about your schedules, financial situation, and vulnerabilities?

Public Records Tell the Story

Government databases and public records provide criminals with detailed information about your family's financial status, property ownership, and legal history. Most of this information is available online for free or for small fees.

Property records reveal your home's value, purchase price, and mortgage information. Court records might contain financial information from divorce proceedings or business disputes. Business registration databases show if family members own companies or have professional licenses.

Voter registration records provide names, addresses, and political affiliations. Professional licensing databases reveal career information and contact details. Even library records and school enrollment information can be accessed through various channels.

Criminals use this public information to build detailed profiles of potential targets and plan convincing social engineering attacks. They might call claiming to be from your mortgage company because they know exactly which bank holds your loan and when you refinanced.

The Business Model of Family-Targeted Crime

Volume Over Value

Most criminals targeting families operate on a volume model: they attack thousands of families hoping for small successes rather than planning elaborate heists against specific targets. This approach requires less skill and preparation but generates steady profits through sheer numbers.

A romance scammer might manage dozens of fake relationships simultaneously, hoping a few victims will send money. A phishing scammer might send millions of fake emails knowing that even a 0.1% success rate generates significant profits.

This volume approach means your family is constantly under attack from multiple criminal groups using different techniques. You might receive phishing emails, phone scams, and social media fraud attempts all in the same week.

The criminals don't need to be sophisticated if they can reach enough potential victims. A simple scam that fools 1 in 1,000 people becomes profitable when sent to millions of families.

Multiple Revenue Streams

Successful attacks on families generate revenue through multiple channels. Criminals don't just steal money directly; they also sell stolen information, use compromised accounts for additional scams, and rent access to infected devices.

Stolen personal information gets sold on criminal marketplaces where other criminals buy it for identity theft, tax fraud, and credit card scams. Medical information sells for particularly high prices because it can be used for insurance fraud and blackmail.

Compromised email accounts become launching pads for scams targeting the victim's contacts. Criminals send fake emergency requests to friends and family, impersonate victims in business communications, and use trusted email addresses to spread malware.

Infected computers join botnets that criminals rent to other operators for cryptocurrency mining, spam distribution, and denial-of-service attacks. Your family's devices might be generating profits for criminals months or years after the initial infection.

> ■ **Danger Zone:** The most profitable attacks are the ones you never discover. Criminals make more money from long-term access to your accounts and devices than from one-time theft of your savings.

Geographic Arbitrage

Many criminal organizations operate from countries where the cost of living is low but internet access is good. This geographic arbitrage allows them to hire skilled workers cheaply and operate with minimal overhead.

A criminal organization in Eastern Europe can live comfortably on profits that would be considered small-time in Western countries. Stealing $5,000 from an American family might represent six months' income for criminals operating from certain countries.

This economic disparity means criminals can invest significant time and resources in attacks against individual families. They can afford to spend weeks researching targets and building convincing scams because the potential payoff represents life-changing money in their local economies.

The global nature of the internet allows these criminals to target victims anywhere in the world while operating from jurisdictions where prosecution is unlikely. They can attack your family from thousands of miles away with minimal risk of legal consequences.

What They Want from Your Family

Financial Information and Access

The primary goal of most family-targeted attacks is accessing your financial accounts and credit information. Criminals want your banking passwords, credit card numbers, Social Security numbers, and any other information that can be converted directly into money.

Online banking credentials give criminals immediate access to your savings and checking accounts. They can transfer money, pay bills to accounts they control, and apply for loans in your name.

Credit card information can be used for fraudulent purchases or sold to other criminals who specialize in card fraud. Full identity packages (name, address, Social Security number, date of birth) sell for $20-$200 on criminal marketplaces.

Investment account access allows criminals to liquidate your retirement savings, stocks, and other investments. They often transfer assets to accounts they control or use your investment accounts to launder money from other crimes.

Personal Information for Identity Theft

Beyond immediate financial theft, criminals want personal information they can use for long-term identity theft. This includes tax records, medical information, employment details, and family relationships.

Tax information allows criminals to file fraudulent tax returns and claim refunds before you file your legitimate return. Medical information can be used for insurance fraud and prescription drug scams.

Employment information helps criminals impersonate you in business contexts and apply for credit using your job history. Family relationship details enable more convincing social engineering attacks against your relatives and colleagues.

Educational records and professional certifications can be used to create fake credentials for other criminal activities. Even seemingly harmless information like your high school mascot or first pet's name can be valuable for bypassing security questions.

Access to Your Network and Devices

Criminals increasingly view compromised family devices as valuable assets in their own right. Your infected laptop becomes a platform for launching attacks against other targets and generating ongoing revenue.

Compromised home networks provide criminals with launching pads for attacks against businesses and organizations. Many companies allow employees to access corporate networks from home, creating opportunities for criminals to reach high-value targets through family devices.

Smart home devices can be recruited into botnets for cryptocurrency mining, distributed denial-of-service attacks, and spam distribution. Criminals rent access to these infected devices to other criminal groups.

Your family's social media accounts and email addresses become tools for spreading malware and scamming your contacts. Criminals use your trusted relationships to launch attacks that would be impossible from unknown accounts.

Knowing who wants to harm your family — and why they see you as a valuable target — is crucial for protecting yourself effectively. These aren't random attacks by amateur criminals; they're systematic operations run by sophisticated organizations that view your family as a profitable business opportunity.

The good news is that understanding their motivations and methods gives you significant advantages in protecting yourself. Once you know how criminals think about targeting families, you can start building defenses that work against real threats.

PART II: Securing your Network

Chapter 3: Your Internet Connection - The Front Door to Everything

When our neighbor used our unsecured wifi for downloading illegal movies

The FBI knocked on our door at 7 AM on a Saturday morning. Two agents in dark suits stood on our porch holding a warrant and asking about our internet connection. Apparently, someone had been using our WiFi network to download copyrighted movies and distribute them to thousands of other people.

"We know the downloads didn't come from your family," the lead agent explained. "Your neighbor has been stealing your internet connection for six months. But legally, you're responsible for everything that happens on your network."

Our neighbor had cracked our WiFi password and turned our internet connection into his personal piracy operation. While we slept, he was downloading terabytes of movies and TV shows through our network. When the entertainment industry's lawyers came after the illegal downloads, they traced the activity back to our address.

We weren't arrested, but we spent three days proving we weren't running a massive piracy ring. The legal bills cost more than a year of internet service. Our neighbor got a slap on the wrist and moved away. We learned that securing your home network isn't just about protecting your family's devices - it's about protecting yourself from other people's crimes.

Your home's internet connection is like the front door to a medieval castle. Everything that protects your family's digital life depends on that first line of defense working properly. But most families leave their castle door wide open with a sign that says "Come on in."

The Castle Analogy: Your Home Network as a Medieval Fortress

Think of your home network like a medieval castle. Your internet connection is the drawbridge that connects your castle to the outside world. Your router is the gatehouse where guards check everyone coming and going. Your WiFi network is the castle walls that keep unwanted visitors out.

Just like a medieval castle, your network security depends on multiple layers of protection working together. Strong walls don't help if the gatehouse guards let everyone pass without checking credentials. Vigilant guards can't protect the castle if the walls have holes in them.

Medieval castles had different areas for different purposes: public courtyards where merchants could trade, private quarters where the family lived, and secure vaults where treasures were stored. Your home network needs the same kind of separation. Guest visitors shouldn't access your family's private devices, and your smart lightbulbs shouldn't connect to the same network as your financial computers.

The castle's defenders knew who belonged inside and who didn't. They could spot intruders and sound alarms when something looked suspicious. You need the same awareness of what's happening on your home network.

But here's where the analogy breaks down: medieval castles only had one drawbridge to defend. Your home network has dozens of wireless devices constantly connecting and disconnecting, each one potentially creating a new entrance for attackers to exploit.

Your Router: The Digital Gatehouse

Your router is the most important security device in your home, but most families treat it like furniture. They plug it in, connect their devices, and never think about it again. That's like hiring guards for your castle gatehouse and then never training them or giving them instructions about who to let inside.

The router controls every piece of information that flows between your home devices and the outside internet. It decides which devices can connect to your network, what websites they can visit, and how they're allowed to communicate with each other. When configured properly, your router becomes a intelligent security guard that protects your family 24/7.

Most internet companies install routers with terrible default security settings because they prioritize easy setup over protection. The default username and password are often printed on a sticker attached to the device. The WiFi network name broadcasts your router manufacturer and model number, telling criminals exactly what vulnerabilities to exploit.

◆ **Personal Experience:** I once drove through a suburban neighborhood with a laptop running network scanning software. In twenty minutes, I found 127 home networks with default passwords, 43 networks with no passwords at all, and dozens of routers that hadn't been updated in years. Any teenager with basic computer skills could have accessed most of these families' internet connections.

Your router probably has dozens of security features that were never activated. Most can block malicious websites, filter inappropriate content, monitor suspicious activity, and alert you when unknown devices try to connect. But these features don't work unless you turn them on and configure them properly.

The router's administrative interface lets you see everything happening on your network: which devices are connected, how much data they're using, what websites they're visiting, and when they're active. This visibility is crucial for spotting problems before they become disasters.

Changing the Default Credentials

The first step in securing any router is changing the default administrative username and password. Criminals have databases containing the default credentials for every router model ever manufactured. If you're still using the factory settings, you're essentially leaving your castle gatehouse unguarded.

Don't just change the password to something slightly different from the default. Choose a completely new username and a strong password that you've never used for anything else. This administrative account controls your entire network, so it deserves the same protection you'd give your banking credentials.

The router's web interface usually requires you to type its IP address into a browser: 192.168.1.1 or 192.168.0.1 for most models. Look for the "Administration," "System," or "Security" section to change the login credentials.

Document the new username and password somewhere safe. You'll need them for future configuration changes, and you don't want to lock yourself out of your own network security controls.

> ★ **Pro Tip:** Use a password manager to generate and store your router credentials. These passwords need to be strong and unique, but you won't be typing them frequently enough to memorize them.

Firmware Updates: Your Digital Castle's Structural Repairs

Router firmware is like the foundation of your castle walls. When security researchers discover vulnerabilities in router software, manufacturers release firmware updates to fix the problems. But unlike your phone or computer, most routers don't update themselves automatically.

Outdated firmware is one of the most common ways criminals gain access to home networks. They scan the internet for routers running vulnerable software versions and exploit known security holes. A router that hasn't been updated in two years probably has dozens of known vulnerabilities that criminals can exploit easily.

Check your router manufacturer's website every six months for firmware updates. Many newer routers handle this automatically or through a companion app — check whether yours does before going the manual route. If you do need to update manually, your manufacturer's support page will walk you through it step by step.

Every manufacturer does this slightly differently, but look for a section labeled "System Update" or "Firmware Upgrade" in your admin interface — that's where it lives on most routers.

> ▲ **Caution:** Never interrupt a firmware update once it starts. If the power goes out or you disconnect the router during an update, you might permanently damage the device and need to replace it entirely.

WiFi Security: Building Strong Castle Walls

Your WiFi network is the wireless boundary of your digital castle. Just like medieval walls, WiFi security depends on both the strength of the barrier and the keys you use to control access through the gates.

Most families set up their WiFi network once and never think about it again. They choose passwords that are easy to remember, use security settings that prioritize convenience over protection, and never monitor who's using their network.

This casual approach to WiFi security creates opportunities for neighbors to steal your internet connection, criminals to access your devices, and attackers to monitor your family's online activities.

WPA3: The Modern Standard for WiFi Protection

WiFi security has evolved through several generations, each stronger than the last. The current best practice is WPA3 (WiFi Protected Access 3), which provides strong encryption and protects against most common attacks.

Older security standards like WEP (Wired Equivalent Privacy) and WPA (original WiFi Protected Access) have known vulnerabilities that criminals can exploit easily. WEP can be cracked in minutes using freely available software. Even WPA2, while still widely used, has weaknesses that sophisticated attackers can exploit.

If your router supports WPA3, use it for all your WiFi networks. If you have older devices that don't support WPA3, consider using WPA2 as a compromise, but plan to upgrade those devices when possible.

The security standard determines how your WiFi password gets converted into encryption keys that protect your wireless communications. Stronger standards make it much more difficult for attackers to intercept and decode your family's wireless traffic.

Choosing Strong WiFi Passwords

Your WiFi password needs to be long, complex, and unrelated to your family's personal information. Criminals can crack short passwords in hours using specialized software and powerful computers.

Avoid using family names, addresses, phone numbers, birthdays, or other personal information in your WiFi password. Criminals research their targets and will try passwords based on information they find about your family online.

The best WiFi passwords are random combinations of letters, numbers, and symbols that are at least 15 characters long. Use your password manager to generate a strong password and store it securely.

Consider using a passphrase instead of a random password: four or five unrelated words combined with numbers and symbols. "Pizza7Elephant!Mountain2Thunder" is easier to remember than "K8#mX9@pL4$vN2!" but just as secure.

A family named the Hendersons lived next to a cemetery and were constantly dealing with teenagers who parked there to drink beer and use their WiFi connection.

The father got tired of changing the WiFi password every few weeks, so he came up with a psychological solution. He named his WiFi network "Cemetery_Surveillance_Camera_05" and set the password to "GhostHunters2024!". The teenagers immediately stopped trying to connect, apparently convinced that the cemetery was monitoring their activities.

The password was quite strong from a technical perspective, but its psychological impact was even more effective than its cryptographic strength. Sometimes the best security solutions combine technical protection with human psychology.

Hiding Your Network Name (SSID)

Your WiFi network broadcasts its name (called the SSID) so that devices can find and connect to it. By default, this name often reveals information about your router model, internet provider, or family name.

Network names like "NETGEAR_5G," "Comcast_Home," or "Smith_Family_WiFi" tell criminals exactly what equipment you're using and help them plan targeted attacks. They can look up known vulnerabilities for your specific router model or use your family name to make social engineering attacks more convincing.

Change your network name to something generic that doesn't reveal personal information about your family or technical details about your equipment. "Home_Network" or "Wireless_Internet" work fine.

You can also configure your router to hide the network name entirely, so it doesn't appear in the list of available WiFi networks. This "security through obscurity" approach won't stop determined attackers, but it reduces the chances that casual criminals or neighbors will target your network.

Hidden networks require you to manually enter the network name when connecting new devices, which adds a small inconvenience but provides an extra layer of protection against opportunistic attacks.

Guest Networks: The Castle's Public Courtyard

Medieval castles had public areas where merchants and visitors could conduct business without accessing the family's private quarters. Your home network needs the same separation between public and private spaces.

A guest network provides internet access for visitors without giving them access to your family's devices, shared files, or private network resources. It's like having a separate entrance to your castle that leads only to the public courtyard.

Most modern routers can create multiple WiFi networks from the same internet connection. Set up one network for your family's devices and another for guests, smart home devices, and any equipment you don't fully trust.

Setting Up Guest Network Isolation

Guest networks should be completely isolated from your main family network. Devices connected to the guest network shouldn't be able to see or communicate with devices on your private network.

This isolation protects your family's computers, phones, and shared storage from potentially compromised guest devices. If a visitor's laptop is infected with malware, the infection can't spread to your family's devices through the network.

Configure the guest network with different security settings than your main network. Use a simpler password that you can share easily with visitors, but make sure the network itself is properly encrypted and isolated.

Set bandwidth limits for the guest network to prevent visitors from consuming all your internet connection. You can usually limit guest users to a percentage of your total bandwidth or set specific speed limits for guest traffic.

★ **Pro Tip:** Change your guest network password monthly and give it a name that makes its purpose obvious, like "VisitorAccess" or "GuestWiFi." This helps you remember which devices should be connecting to which network.

What Goes on the Guest Network

Use the guest network for any device that doesn't need access to your family's private resources. This includes visitor devices, smart home gadgets, gaming consoles, streaming devices, and anything you consider less trustworthy than your family's primary computers and phones.

Smart home devices are particularly good candidates for guest network isolation. Your smart doorbell doesn't need to access your family's photos, and your smart thermostat doesn't need to communicate with your laptop. Putting these devices on a separate network prevents them from becoming gateways to your family's private information.

Some families put all their Internet of Things (IoT) devices on the guest network as a security measure. This approach treats smart home devices like untrusted visitors that deserve internet access but shouldn't be allowed into your family's private digital space.

Network Monitoring: Keeping Watch From the Castle Walls

Medieval castle guards kept constant watch for approaching threats and suspicious activity around the fortress. You need the same awareness of what's happening on your home network.

Most families have no idea what devices are connected to their network or what those devices are doing online. They assume everything is working properly until something obviously breaks or gets compromised.

This blind trust in network activity is like having castle guards who sleep through their shifts. Attackers count on families not paying attention to unusual network activity or unauthorized device connections.

Knowing What's Connected

Check your router's administrative interface monthly to see what's connected. Most routers show this under "Connected Devices," "Device List," or "DHCP Clients" — the label varies by brand, but the list shows everything currently on your network.

Look for devices you don't recognize. Unknown devices might indicate that neighbors are stealing your WiFi, criminals have gained access to your network, or family members have connected new devices without telling you.

Pay attention to device names that seem suspicious or out of place. Attackers sometimes try to hide compromised devices by giving them names that sound like legitimate network equipment.

Some routers can send notifications when new devices connect to your network. Enable these alerts so you'll know immediately when unauthorized devices attempt to join your WiFi network.

◆ **Personal Experience:** I discovered that my neighbor's teenager had been using my WiFi for months when I noticed a gaming console connected to my network at 3 AM every night. The kid had guessed my password and was downloading games while his parents slept. He'd been doing it for so long that he'd consumed nearly half my monthly data allowance.

Monitoring Data Usage

Unusual data usage patterns can indicate network compromises or unauthorized activity. If your internet connection suddenly becomes slow or you exceed your data limits without explanation, someone might be using your network for activities you didn't authorize.

Check your router's traffic monitoring features to see which devices are using the most data. Look for unexpected spikes in usage, especially during times when your family isn't actively using the internet.

Infected devices often generate unusual network traffic as they communicate with criminal servers, download additional malware, or participate in botnet activities. A computer that's suddenly using gigabytes of data overnight might be compromised.

Some routers can block internet access for specific devices or set usage limits for individual devices. These features help you investigate suspicious activity without affecting your family's normal internet use.

Recognizing Attack Patterns

Learn to recognize common signs of network attacks and compromises. Multiple failed login attempts against your router's administrative interface might indicate that criminals are trying to guess your credentials.

Devices that connect to your network and immediately start scanning for other devices are probably looking for vulnerabilities to exploit. Legitimate devices usually connect to the internet without probing other network resources.

Network traffic to suspicious websites or IP addresses might indicate compromised devices communicating with criminal servers. Many routers can log web traffic and alert you to connections with known malicious destinations.

> ▲ **Caution:** Don't assume that network problems are always caused by equipment failures or internet service issues. Sometimes slow connections, frequent disconnections, and unusual behavior indicate security compromises.

Advanced Router Security Features

Modern routers include security features that most families never activate. These tools can automatically block malicious websites, filter inappropriate content, and detect suspicious network activity.

Content Filtering and Parental Controls

Router-level content filtering works for all devices on your network, not just computers with filtering software installed. You can block categories of websites, specific domains, or internet access during certain hours.

These features are particularly useful for protecting children's devices that might not have their own filtering software. Tablets, gaming consoles, and smart TVs often lack solid parental control options, but router-level filtering affects all network traffic.

Set up different filtering rules for different devices or network users. Your children's devices might need strict content filtering, while adult devices get unrestricted access.

Time-based restrictions can automatically disable internet access for specific devices during homework time, meals, or bedtime. These controls work even if children try to circumvent restrictions on their individual devices.

Intrusion Detection and Prevention

Some routers can detect and block common network attacks automatically. These intrusion detection systems monitor network traffic for suspicious patterns and block connections that match known attack signatures.

Enable these features if your router supports them, but understand their limitations. Intrusion detection works best against known attack patterns and might not catch sophisticated or novel attacks.

These systems can generate false positives, blocking legitimate network traffic that happens to match attack signatures. Monitor the blocked connections log to make sure important services aren't being blocked unnecessarily.

VPN Server Capabilities

Many modern routers can act as VPN servers, allowing your family to securely access your home network from remote locations. This feature creates an encrypted tunnel between your devices and your home network when you're using public WiFi or traveling.

Setting up a home VPN server lets you access your home network's resources securely from anywhere in the world. You can reach shared files, printers, and other network devices as if you were at home.

This capability also provides an extra layer of security when using public WiFi networks. Instead of trusting airport or coffee shop internet connections, you can route all your traffic through your secured home network.

> ■ **Danger Zone:** Misconfigured VPN servers can create security vulnerabilities that allow attackers to access your home network from the internet. Only enable VPN server features if you understand how to configure them securely.

Your home network is the foundation of your family's digital security. Like the walls and gatehouse of a medieval castle, router security determines whether everything else you do to protect your family will succeed or fail.

The time you invest in properly configuring your router and monitoring your network will pay dividends for years. A well-secured home network automatically protects every device your family connects to it and provides early warning when something goes wrong.

But network security is just the foundation. The devices you connect to that network bring their own vulnerabilities and risks that need to be addressed individually.

Chapter 4: Smart Home Devices - When Convenience Becomes Dangerous

---

The baby monitor that strangers were watching and talking through

---

Three-year-old Emma was having trouble sleeping when her parents heard a man's voice coming through the baby monitor speaker: "Wake up, little girl. I'm watching you."

The Richardsons rushed to Emma's room, expecting to find an intruder. Instead, they found their daughter alone, pointing at the baby monitor camera that was slowly panning back and forth across her room. A stranger had gained access to their "smart" baby monitor and was using it to spy on their child and terrorize their family.

The voice continued as they stood there in shock: "I can see you now, mommy and daddy. Your daughter is very pretty."

They ripped the monitor's power cord from the wall, but the damage was done. A criminal had been watching their child sleep, possibly for weeks or months. The device they'd bought to keep Emma safe had become a window for predators to access their most private family moments.

The baby monitor wasn't malfunctioning. It was working exactly as designed, with one fatal flaw: it had no meaningful security protection. The default password was "admin," the encryption was easily broken, and anyone with basic computer skills could access thousands of these monitors from anywhere in the world.

Your home is probably filled with smart devices that have the same vulnerabilities. Each one was designed to make your life more convenient, but together they've turned your house into a surveillance system that you don't control.

The Smart Home Security Paradox

Smart home devices promise to make your house safer and more convenient. Smart locks protect your doors. Security cameras monitor your property. Smart doorbells let you see who's visiting. Smart speakers give you instant access to information and emergency services.

But these same devices often make your home less secure than it was before you installed them. They create new entry points for criminals, new ways for strangers to spy on your family, and new methods for attackers to disrupt your daily life.

The security paradox exists because smart home manufacturers prioritize convenience and low prices over security and privacy. They assume most families will never change default settings, so they design devices that work immediately out of the box with minimal configuration.

This approach treats security as an optional feature for advanced users rather than a fundamental requirement for every device. The result is millions of smart home devices with weak passwords, poor encryption, and obvious vulnerabilities that criminals exploit routinely.

> ◆ **Personal Experience:** I tested the security of smart home devices at a cybersecurity conference by setting up a fake wireless network called "Free Conference WiFi." Within an hour, I'd captured login credentials from seventeen different smart devices as conference attendees connected them to my network. Most people had no idea their devices were automatically sharing passwords and personal information with anyone who could mimic a WiFi network.

The fundamental problem is that most smart home devices are just small computers disguised as appliances. They run operating systems, connect to the internet, and contain many of the same vulnerabilities as laptops and servers. But families treat them like traditional appliances that never need security updates or configuration changes.

Security Cameras and Video Doorbells: When Watchers Get Watched

Home security cameras and video doorbells are supposed to protect your family by recording criminal activity and deterring intruders. Instead, they often become tools that criminals use to spy on your family and plan attacks.

The irony is brutal: devices designed to catch criminals often help criminals catch you. Insecure security cameras give attackers real-time intelligence about your family's routines, valuables, and vulnerabilities.

The Default Password Problem

Most security cameras ship with default usernames and passwords printed in the manual or on a sticker attached to the device. Common combinations include admin/admin, admin/password, or admin/123456. Manufacturers assume you'll change these credentials during setup, but most families never do.

Criminals have automated tools that scan the internet for security cameras using default passwords. These tools can find and access thousands of cameras in minutes, creating massive databases of compromised surveillance systems.

Once criminals access your camera's administrative interface, they can watch live video feeds, download recorded footage, change camera settings, and even disable the device entirely. Some cameras allow remote access to other devices on your home network through the camera's built-in web server.

The Petrov family discovered their camera was compromised when neighbors told them their video doorbell was talking to visitors. Criminals had accessed the device and were using its two-way audio feature to harass delivery drivers and solicitors.

The harassment continued for weeks because the family didn't know how to change the camera's password or check its access logs.

Cloud Storage Vulnerabilities

Many security cameras automatically upload recorded footage to cloud storage services controlled by the manufacturer. This cloud storage often has weaker security than the cameras themselves, creating opportunities for massive data breaches.

When criminals hack camera manufacturer servers, they gain access to video footage from thousands of homes simultaneously. These breaches have exposed intimate family moments, private conversations, and detailed intelligence about families' daily routines.

The Zimmerman family learned about cloud storage risks when their camera manufacturer suffered a data breach that exposed six months of video recordings from their home. The leaked footage included private conversations about family finances, arguments between parents, and video of their teenage daughter changing clothes in her bedroom.

Cloud storage also creates ongoing privacy risks even when there are no security breaches. Camera manufacturers often retain the right to access your video footage for "quality improvement" and "technical support" purposes. Your family's private moments might be reviewed by company employees in countries with different privacy laws than your own.

> ★ **Pro Tip:** Set up local storage for security cameras whenever possible. Many cameras can record to local network drives or SD cards instead of cloud storage, giving you complete control over who can access your family's video footage.

Securing Camera Systems

Change default passwords immediately after installing any security camera. Use strong, unique passwords that you've never used for other accounts. Camera passwords should be at least 15 characters long and contain a mix of letters, numbers, and symbols.

Enable two-factor authentication if your camera supports it. This feature requires you to enter a code from your phone or email in addition to your password when accessing the camera remotely.

Update camera firmware regularly. Security researchers frequently discover vulnerabilities in camera software, and manufacturers release updates to fix these problems. Cameras that haven't been updated in six months probably have known security holes that criminals can exploit.

Review your camera's privacy settings and disable features you don't need. Many cameras can recognize faces, track movement across multiple cameras, and analyze audio for specific keywords. These advanced features create additional privacy risks without providing meaningful security benefits for most families.

Disable remote access features unless you absolutely need them. Cameras that can't be accessed from the internet can't be hacked from the internet. If you need remote monitoring capabilities, set up a VPN connection to your home network instead of exposing cameras directly to internet access.

The most secure camera installation I ever saw belonged to a paranoid security consultant who had learned from bitter experience. He ran all camera cables through locked conduits, powered cameras from a central uninterruptible power supply, and recorded everything to a hidden server that wasn't connected to the internet.

His cameras had no wireless connectivity, no cloud storage, and no remote access features. The only way to view footage was to physically access the hidden server room in his basement. When burglars broke into his garage, they had no idea they were being recorded because there was no way for them to detect or compromise his camera system.

The installation wasn't convenient for daily use, but it was absolutely secure. He could prove in court exactly what the burglars had stolen without worrying that criminals might have disabled his cameras or accessed his footage.

Smart Speakers: Always Listening, Sometimes Recording

Smart speakers like Amazon Echo, Google Home, and Apple HomePod are designed to listen constantly for wake words like "Alexa," "Hey Google," or "Hey Siri." This always-on listening creates privacy risks that most families don't understand or consider.

The Listening Problem

Smart speakers record and analyze every sound in your home to detect wake words. Manufacturers claim these devices only send audio to their servers after hearing the wake word, but the reality is more complicated.

The devices frequently misinterpret ordinary conversation as wake words and begin recording private conversations. Background noise, television shows, and even conversations in foreign languages can trigger recordings that get uploaded to company servers without your knowledge.

Amazon admitted that its Echo devices have recorded thousands of private conversations accidentally. Google revealed that contractors regularly review Home device recordings to improve voice recognition accuracy. Apple acknowledged that Siri recordings are analyzed by human reviewers who can hear intimate personal details.

The Valencia family discovered their smart speaker's privacy problems when they received targeted advertisements for medical treatments related to a private conversation about their son's learning disability. The family had never searched for this information online, but their smart speaker had apparently recorded their discussion and shared it with advertising companies.

Voice Profile Security

Smart speakers create voice profiles for family members to provide personalized responses and restrict access to certain features. But these voice profiles can be spoiled by recordings of your family's voices or sophisticated audio generation tools.

Children's voices are particularly easy to spoof because they're higher-pitched and less distinctive than adult voices. Criminals can use recordings from social media videos, school presentations, or playground activities to generate fake voice commands that smart speakers accept as legitimate.

The Rodriguez family learned about voice spoofing when their neighbor's teenager used recordings from their daughter's TikTok videos to control their smart home system. The teen could unlock doors, disable security systems, and access personal information just by playing manipulated audio files near their smart speaker.

Voice profiles also create privacy risks within families. Parents might restrict certain features for children, but smart speakers can't always distinguish between family members' voices accurately. Children can often access restricted content or make unauthorized purchases by speaking in different tones or accents.

Smart Speaker Security Settings

Review your smart speaker's privacy settings and disable features you don't need. Most devices can function without creating voice profiles, storing conversation history, or sharing usage data with advertising companies.

Delete voice recordings regularly. Amazon, Google, and Apple all provide options to delete stored recordings, but the process isn't automatic. Set calendar reminders to clean out your voice history every month.

Disable purchasing through voice commands. Smart speakers can place orders, make payments, and authorize transactions based on voice commands alone. These features are convenient but create opportunities for accidental purchases or voice spoofing attacks.

> ▲ **Caution:** Muting smart speakers doesn't prevent them from being accessed remotely if criminals have compromised your home network. A truly private conversation requires either removing the devices from the room or disconnecting them from the internet entirely.

Use the physical mute button when discussing sensitive topics. Most smart speakers have hardware mute switches that physically disconnect the microphones. Use these switches during private conversations about finances, health, legal matters, or family problems.

Smart Appliances: The Unexpected Internet Connections

Modern appliances connect to the internet for features that seem innocent but create unexpected security and privacy risks. Your smart refrigerator, washing machine, and coffee maker are all tiny computers that can be hacked, monitored, and used to attack other devices.

Refrigerators and Kitchen Appliances

Smart refrigerators can connect to your email accounts to display calendar appointments and shopping lists on their built-in screens. This email access creates opportunities for criminals to read your personal correspondence and gain intelligence about your family's schedules and activities.

The Martinez family discovered their refrigerator's email vulnerabilities when they noticed their spam folder contained emails they'd never seen. Their smart refrigerator had been compromised and was being used to send spam messages to thousands of recipients. The refrigerator's email account had been added to criminal mailing lists, and the device was automatically sending malware to everyone in the family's contact list.

Smart coffee makers and kitchen appliances often contain hidden cameras and microphones for "user experience research." These sensors can record conversations in your kitchen and monitor your family's eating habits without obvious indication that recording is taking place.

Some smart ovens can be controlled remotely through smartphone apps, creating opportunities for criminals to preheat ovens, change cooking temperatures, or disable safety features. These attacks could cause fires, food poisoning, or carbon monoxide exposure.

Washing Machines and Utility Appliances

Smart washing machines and dryers connect to the internet to send notifications when cycles complete and optimize energy usage based on utility rates. But these connections also provide criminals with intelligence about your family's routines and when you're home.

Laundry patterns reveal personal information about family size, lifestyle, and schedules. Criminals can determine when families are on vacation by monitoring smart appliance activity patterns. A washing machine that's inactive for two weeks indicates an empty house.

> ■ **Danger Zone:** Smart appliances often have access to your home's utility systems and can potentially cause physical damage if compromised. A hacked water heater could overheat and explode. A compromised smart stove could start a fire.

The Hassan family's smart water heater was compromised and used as part of a botnet for cryptocurrency mining. The heater's computer processor was powerful enough to perform complex calculations, and criminals used the device to generate digital currency while driving up the family's electricity bills.

Smart thermostats collect detailed information about your family's presence in different rooms and your preferred temperature settings. This data reveals which rooms are occupied at what times, when family members sleep, and when the house is empty.

Unexpected Connectivity in Traditional Appliances

Many appliances that don't advertise internet connectivity still contain wireless chips for diagnostic purposes or future feature updates. Your "dumb" appliances might be smarter than you think.

Appliance repair technicians use wireless connections to diagnose problems, update software, and configure device settings. These service connections often remain active after repair visits, creating permanent internet access that most families don't know exists.

Some appliances connect to cellular networks instead of WiFi, bypassing your home network security entirely. These cellular connections are often controlled by appliance manufacturers or service companies rather than your family.

◆ **Personal Experience:** I conducted a security audit for a family who complained about mysterious network activity on their home router. After checking every computer, phone, and obvious smart device, we discovered their two-year-old microwave was connecting to WiFi and downloading software updates. The microwave had never been set up for internet access, but it was using a neighbor's unsecured network to phone home to the manufacturer every night.

The Morrison family discovered their "offline" dishwasher was transmitting data when their internet bill included charges for a device they'd never connected to their network. The dishwasher had a hidden cellular modem that reported usage statistics and diagnostic information to the manufacturer continuously.

Regular Maintenance: Keeping Smart Devices Secure

Smart home devices need regular security maintenance just like computers and phones. But most families install these devices and never think about them again, assuming they'll work safely forever without updates or configuration changes.

This "set it and forget it" approach to smart home security creates opportunities for criminals to exploit vulnerabilities that remain unpatched for months or years. Devices that were secure when first installed become vulnerable as criminals discover new attack methods and manufacturers release security updates.

Software Updates and Firmware Patches

Check for software updates on all smart home devices at least quarterly. Many devices don't update automatically and require manual intervention to install security patches.

The update process varies by device type and manufacturer. Some devices can download updates through their smartphone apps, while others require you to access web-based administrative interfaces or download firmware files from manufacturer websites.

Create a calendar reminder to check for updates on the first day of each season. This quarterly schedule ensures that critical security patches get installed within a reasonable time frame without requiring daily maintenance.

Document the software versions and update history for all your smart devices. This record helps you track which devices have been updated recently and identify devices that might have been abandoned by their manufacturers.

Password Rotation and Access Reviews

Change passwords on smart home devices annually or whenever you suspect a security compromise. Use your password manager to generate strong, unique passwords for each device.

Review user accounts and access permissions for all smart devices. Remove accounts for family members who no longer live in your home and revoke access for any service technicians or contractors who no longer need access to your systems.

Check the activity logs for devices that support this feature. Look for unusual access patterns, failed login attempts, or connections from unexpected locations.

Some smart devices create temporary access codes for service technicians or delivery personnel. Review these temporary codes regularly and delete any that are no longer needed.

Network Monitoring for Smart Devices

Monitor your home network to identify smart devices that are communicating unexpectedly with internet servers. Use your router's traffic monitoring features to spot devices that are uploading large amounts of data or connecting to suspicious destinations.

Pay attention to smart devices that suddenly start consuming more bandwidth than usual. Compromised devices often generate unusual network traffic as they communicate with criminal servers or participate in botnet activities.

Some routers can alert you when smart devices attempt to communicate with known malicious websites or IP addresses. Enable these security features if your router supports them.

> ★ **Pro Tip:** Set up a separate network specifically for smart home devices and monitor its traffic carefully. This isolation makes it easier to spot unusual activity and prevents compromised smart devices from accessing your family's computers and phones.

Consider using a network monitoring tool specifically designed for smart home devices. These tools can identify all the smart devices on your network and alert you to unusual behavior or security vulnerabilities.

End-of-Life Planning for Smart Devices

Plan for the eventual replacement of smart home devices before they become security liabilities. Most manufacturers only provide security updates for three to five years after a device is released.

Research the support lifecycle for smart devices before purchasing them. Choose manufacturers with strong track records of providing long-term security updates and clear end-of-life policies.

Replace smart devices that are no longer receiving security updates, even if they're still functioning properly. Unsupported devices become increasingly vulnerable as criminals discover new attack methods.

Properly dispose of old smart devices by factory resetting them and removing them from your network before discarding or donating them. Many devices store WiFi passwords and other sensitive information that should be wiped before disposal.

Smart home devices can make your family's life more convenient and potentially more secure, but only if you treat them as the internet-connected computers they really are. They need the same security attention you give to laptops and smartphones: strong passwords, regular updates, careful monitoring, and eventual replacement when they're no longer supported.

The convenience these devices provide isn't worth the risks they create unless you're willing to invest the time and effort needed to secure them properly. Your family's safety and privacy depend on understanding that every smart device is a potential entry point for criminals and a possible window into your most private moments.

PART III: Protecting your Computing Devices

Chapter 5: Computers and Laptops - Your Family's Work Stations

---

The computer with 496 viruses - "The owner had no idea it was infected"

I walked into the computer repair shop expecting a routine virus cleanup. The customer had complained that his laptop was "running a little slow" and thought it might need a tune-up. What I found was the most infected computer I'd ever encountered in twenty years of IT work.

The security scan took three hours to complete and found 496 separate pieces of malware. The computer had seventeen different viruses, forty-three spyware programs, and dozens of browser hijackers. Criminal software was stealing passwords, recording keystrokes, taking screenshots, and turning the webcam on and off randomly.

The owner sat next to me, stunned, as I showed him the scan results. "But I have antivirus software," he kept saying. He did, but it was three years out of date and hadn't been updated since he bought the computer. The criminals had been living in his laptop for months, stealing his personal information and using his computer to attack other victims.

The worst part? He'd been using this infected computer for online banking, tax preparation, and work email. Every password he'd typed, every document he'd opened, and every website he'd visited had been recorded and transmitted to criminal servers. His laptop had become a window that criminals used to watch every aspect of his digital life.

Most families have at least one computer that's almost as badly infected as this one. You just don't know it yet because modern malware hides itself carefully and doesn't slow down your computer enough to be obvious.

Windows 11 Security Essentials: Building Your Digital Foundation

Windows computers are the primary targets for most cybercriminals because they're the most common operating system in homes and businesses. The good news is that Windows 11 includes powerful security features that can protect your family effectively. The bad news is that most of these features are buried in settings menus that most people never explore.

Windows Defender: The Built-In Guardian

Windows 11 comes with Microsoft Defender Antivirus built into the operating system. This isn't the weak, optional antivirus software that came with older Windows versions. Modern Windows Defender is a sophisticated security system that provides real-time protection against malware, ransomware, and other threats.

Windows Defender updates automatically multiple times per day and uses cloud-based intelligence to identify new threats faster than traditional antivirus software. It integrates deeply with the operating system to detect and block attacks that other security software might miss.

The best part about Windows Defender is that it requires no subscription fees, configuration, or maintenance. It just works silently in the background, protecting your computer without slowing it down or bombarding you with advertising for premium upgrades.

> ◆ **Personal Experience:** I conducted a security test comparing Windows Defender to four commercial antivirus products. Windows Defender detected 99.2% of malware samples and had the lowest false positive rate of any product tested. It also used less system memory and processor power than most commercial alternatives, making computers run faster rather than slower.

Many families disable Windows Defender to install third-party antivirus software, often making their computers less secure in the process. Unless you have specific requirements that Windows Defender can't meet, there's no need to replace it with commercial alternatives.

User Account Control: Your Security Checkpoint

User Account Control (UAC) is the feature that dims your screen and asks "Do you want to allow this app to make changes to your device?" when programs try to modify system settings. Most people find these prompts annoying and click "Yes" without reading them, but UAC is one of Windows' most important security features.

UAC prevents malware from making system-level changes without your explicit permission. When criminals try to install backdoors, disable security software, or modify critical system files, UAC forces them to ask for your approval first.

The prompts can be annoying, but they're your early warning system for potential malware infections. If you see UAC prompts appearing when you haven't installed new software or changed system settings, your computer might be infected.

Never disable UAC entirely, even if the prompts seem inconvenient. You can adjust the sensitivity level to reduce false alarms, but completely disabling UAC removes a critical security barrier that protects your computer from automated attacks.

Configure UAC to always prompt for administrator credentials, even if you're logged in as an administrator. This setting forces you to consciously approve system changes instead of allowing them to happen automatically.

Windows Updates: Your Security Lifeline

Windows Update delivers security patches that fix vulnerabilities before criminals can exploit them. Microsoft releases security updates on the second Tuesday of each month, with emergency patches released when critical vulnerabilities are discovered.

Enable automatic updates for Windows and configure your computer to install them immediately. Delaying security updates gives criminals time to exploit known vulnerabilities that Microsoft has already fixed.

Schedule automatic restarts for times when your family isn't using the computer. Many security updates require restarts to become effective, and postponing these restarts leaves your computer vulnerable to attacks.

Monitor Windows Update history to ensure updates are installing successfully. Failed updates can leave your computer vulnerable to attacks that should have been prevented by recent security patches.

A small business owner kept postponing security updates because they "interrupted his work." He postponed updates for three months, claiming he was too busy to restart his computer.

Criminals eventually exploited a vulnerability that Microsoft had patched two months earlier. The attack encrypted all the business files and demanded $50,000 ransom. The owner paid the ransom but never received the decryption keys. He lost three years of customer data and had to rebuild his entire business from scratch.

The tragedy was completely preventable. A simple restart to install security updates would have protected his computer from the attack. His refusal to spend ten minutes installing updates cost him his entire business.

BitLocker Drive Encryption: Protecting Your Data

Think of BitLocker as a deadbolt on your hard drive. If someone steals your laptop, they get a box of useless encrypted data. Without the password, nothing on that drive is readable — not your photos, not your bank statements, not your tax returns.

Turn it on, let it run overnight, and forget about it. BitLocker encrypts in the background and doesn't slow down everyday use once it's done. Windows Pro and Enterprise include it automatically; if you're on Windows Home, look for "Device Encryption" in Settings — it's the same protection under a different name.

> ★ **Pro Tip:** Enable BitLocker before storing sensitive information on new computers. Encrypting a drive that already contains files takes much longer than encrypting an empty drive during initial setup.

Store your BitLocker recovery key in a safe location separate from your computer. If you forget your password or the computer's hardware fails, the recovery key is the only way to access your encrypted files.

On computers more than five or six years old, BitLocker can make things noticeably slower. If that's you, it's still worth turning on — just know it might be time to start thinking about an upgrade.

macOS Security for Home Users: The Walled Garden Approach

Mac computers have earned a reputation for being more secure than Windows machines, but this reputation is partly based on market share rather than superior security design. As Macs become more popular, criminals are investing more effort in developing Mac-specific attacks.

System Integrity Protection: The Mac's Digital Immune System

macOS includes System Integrity Protection (SIP), which prevents malware from modifying critical system files and processes. SIP creates a protected zone around the operating system that even administrator users can't modify without special tools.

This protection makes it much harder for malware to establish persistent infections or disable security features. Even if criminals gain administrator access to your Mac, they can't modify the core operating system files that would give them permanent control.

SIP is enabled by default and should never be disabled unless you have specific technical requirements. Some software installation guides suggest disabling SIP temporarily, but this creates serious security risks that outweigh any convenience benefits.

Gatekeeper: Your App Security Bouncer

Gatekeeper prevents your Mac from running software that hasn't been signed by registered Apple developers. This code signing system makes it much harder for criminals to distribute malware through fake applications or infected downloads.

When you try to run unsigned software, Gatekeeper displays warnings and requires you to explicitly approve the application before it will run. These warnings help prevent accidental malware infections from downloading and running suspicious programs.

Don't bypass Gatekeeper warnings unless you're absolutely certain the software is legitimate and necessary. Right-clicking applications and selecting "Open" to bypass Gatekeeper warnings should be reserved for software from trusted developers that you've specifically chosen to install.

Keep Gatekeeper enabled on the highest security setting: "App Store and identified developers." This setting provides the best protection against malware while still allowing you to install legitimate software from sources outside the App Store.

FileVault Full Disk Encryption

FileVault does for Macs what BitLocker does for Windows — it locks the hard drive so that a stolen computer is a doorstop. The encryption happens invisibly; you won't notice any difference in day-to-day use.

Find it under System Settings → Privacy & Security → FileVault. Turn it on, let your Mac run overnight, and it's done. Newer Macs with Apple Silicon chips encrypt by default if you set a login password — you may already be protected.

Store your FileVault recovery key securely and separately from your computer. Apple can store the recovery key in your iCloud account, but consider printing a copy and storing it in a safe location for maximum security.

Check once a year that FileVault is still on — major macOS updates occasionally reset it. Thirty seconds in System Settings confirms everything is still locked down.

Safari Security Settings

Safari includes strong security features that protect against malicious websites and prevent unauthorized downloads.

Enable "Warn when visiting a fraudulent website" and "Block pop-up windows" to reduce exposure to common web-based attacks.

Disable Java and Flash plugins in Safari unless you specifically need them for trusted websites. These plugins are common targets for criminal exploitation and aren't necessary for most modern web browsing.

> ▲ **Caution:** Mac security relies heavily on users making good decisions about what software to install and what websites to trust. The operating system's security features can't protect against social engineering attacks that trick users into voluntarily installing malware.

Configure Safari to ask before downloading files and to automatically delete downloads after one day. This setting prevents criminals from filling your computer with malware disguised as legitimate downloads.

Use Safari's private browsing mode when accessing sensitive websites or entering personal information on unfamiliar sites. Private browsing prevents websites from storing tracking information and reduces the risk of session hijacking attacks.

Shared Computer Best Practices: Managing Multiple Users Safely

Family computers shared by multiple users create unique security challenges. Children download games that might contain malware. Teenagers visit websites that parents wouldn't approve. Adults use the same computer for both entertainment and financial transactions.

User Account Separation: Digital Bedroom Doors

Create separate user accounts for each family member who uses shared computers. Each account should have its own password, settings, and file storage area that other users can't access without permission.

Set up children's accounts as standard users rather than administrators. Standard user accounts can't install software, change system settings, or access other users' files without administrator approval.

Reserve administrator accounts for adults who need to install software and manage system settings. Use administrator accounts only for administrative tasks, not for daily web browsing or entertainment activities.

Configure parental controls for children's accounts to restrict access to inappropriate websites and prevent installation of unauthorized software. These controls work at the operating system level and can't be bypassed easily by tech-savvy children.

Log out of user accounts when switching between users instead of using fast user switching. Logging out completely closes all programs and clears sensitive information from memory, preventing other users from accessing previously opened files or websites.

Shared Storage Security

Encrypt shared folders that contain sensitive family information: tax documents, medical records, financial statements, and private photos. Both Windows and macOS can create encrypted folders that require passwords to access.

Create separate shared folders for different types of content: family photos that everyone can access, financial documents that only adults can view, and work files that only specific family members need.

Back up shared computers more frequently than single-user computers. Multiple users create more opportunities for accidental file deletion, malware infection, and system corruption.

Use cloud storage with careful access controls for files that multiple family members need to access from different devices. Services like iCloud, Google Drive, and OneDrive allow you to share specific folders while keeping other files private.

Browsing Safety for Shared Computers

Configure web browsers to automatically delete browsing history, cookies, and temporary files when closed. This setting prevents family members from accessing each other's browsing history and reduces the risk of session hijacking attacks.

Install browser extensions that block malicious websites and filter inappropriate content. Extensions like uBlock Origin and Malwarebytes Browser Guard work for all users on shared computers.

> ■ **Danger Zone:** Never save banking passwords or credit card information on shared computers. Other family members, repair technicians, or criminals who gain access to the computer can steal this information easily.

Disable password saving in web browsers on shared computers. Saved passwords can be accessed by other users and create security risks if the computer is stolen or compromised.

Use private browsing mode for all sensitive activities: online banking, shopping, and accessing personal accounts. Private browsing prevents other users from accessing your session information and reduces tracking by websites.

Physical Security in the Home: Protecting Against Theft and Tampering

Digital security is worthless if criminals can physically access your computers. Home break-ins, curious visitors, and even family members can compromise your computer security by accessing devices directly.

Laptop Theft Prevention

Secure laptops when not in use, even in your own home. Visitors, repair technicians, and household workers have opportunities to steal portable computers that are left unattended.

Use cable locks to secure laptops to desks or tables when working in public areas of your home. Cable locks won't stop determined thieves with bolt cutters, but they prevent opportunistic theft during brief absences.

Encrypt laptop hard drives and require passwords to wake from sleep mode. These settings make stolen laptops worthless to criminals who can't access the encrypted files.

Store laptops in unexpected locations when traveling or when the house will be empty for extended periods. Criminals look for computers in obvious places like home offices and bedroom desks.

Desktop Computer Security

Position desktop computers so that screens aren't visible through windows. Criminals case houses before burglaries and look for valuable electronics that justify the risk of breaking in.

Secure computer towers in locked cabinets or cable them to heavy furniture. Desktop computers are easier targets than laptops because they're usually left in predictable locations.

Use privacy screens on monitors if your computer is visible to visitors or household workers. Privacy screens prevent shoulder surfing and keep sensitive information private when others are in the room.

Hide external hard drives and backup devices in separate locations from the computers they protect. Criminals who steal computers often take visible storage devices as well, defeating backup strategies that keep everything in the same location.

Access Control in the Home

Lock computer rooms or home offices when the house is empty or when workers are present for repairs or maintenance. Many home burglaries are committed by people who have legitimate reasons to be in your house.

Change computer passwords immediately after house guests, repair technicians, or household workers have had access to areas where computers are located. These people might have observed you entering passwords or accessing sensitive information.

Cover webcams when not in use to prevent unauthorized recording. Simple tape or webcam covers provide physical protection against malware that might activate cameras remotely.

Secure backup devices and external storage in fireproof safes or safety deposit boxes. Physical security for backups is as important as digital security for the data they protect.

Cleaning and Maintenance Security

Supervise repair technicians and never leave them alone with computers that contain sensitive information. Criminals sometimes pose as repair workers to gain access to homes and computers.

Remove hard drives from computers before disposing of them or donating them to charity. Deleting files doesn't remove them from hard drives, and criminals can recover sensitive information from computers you thought were wiped clean.

Use secure deletion software to overwrite hard drives multiple times before disposal. Simple deletion leaves recoverable data that criminals can extract using specialized software.

Physically destroy hard drives that contained extremely sensitive information before throwing them away. Drilling holes through the platters or degaussing with powerful magnets ensures that data can't be recovered.

◆ **Personal Experience:** I once helped a family whose identity was stolen after they donated an old computer to charity. They'd deleted their files and thought the computer was clean, but criminals who bought the computer from the charity were able to recover five years of tax returns, bank statements, and personal photos. The recovered information was used for identity theft that cost the family $15,000 and two years of credit repair work.

Computers and laptops are the foundation of your family's digital life. They store your most important files, provide access to your financial accounts, and connect you to the outside world. Securing these devices properly protects everything else you do online.

The time you invest in configuring security settings, creating proper user accounts, and implementing physical security measures will protect your family from both digital and physical threats. But remember that computer security is just one layer of protection in your family's overall security plan.

Chapter 6: Phones and Tablets - Your Most Personal Information

---

Sally left her tablet "just for a minute" and lost access to all her accounts

---

Sally Brennan stepped away from her table at the coffee shop for thirty seconds to grab napkins. When she returned, her iPad was gone. The thief had vanished into the crowd, taking with him access to Sally's email, banking apps, social media accounts, and thousands of family photos.

The tablet wasn't protected by a passcode because Sally found it "annoying to type numbers every time." Her banking app was set to log in automatically. Her email stayed open constantly. Her photo library synced to all her devices. In thirty seconds, a stranger had gained access to her entire digital life.

Within an hour, the thief had transferred $3,200 from her checking account, changed her email password to lock her out of recovery options, and posted embarrassing photos from her private collection to her social media accounts. He'd also accessed her work email and sent inappropriate messages to her colleagues and clients.

The financial theft was bad enough, but the personal violation was devastating. The thief had access to private conversations with her husband, medical information about her children, and intimate photos from family vacations. He used this information to harass Sally and demand additional payments to stop releasing more private content.

Sally's thirty-second lapse in attention cost her $3,200, her job, and months of effort to regain control of her accounts. A simple passcode would have prevented the entire disaster, but she'd chosen convenience over security and paid a terrible price.

Your phone contains more personal information than your wallet, your diary, and your home computer combined. It knows where you sleep, work, and shop. It has photos of your family, access to your bank accounts, and records of every conversation you've had. Yet most people protect their phones less carefully than they protect their house keys.

Smartphone Security: Protecting Your Digital Life

Your smartphone is the most valuable target in your pocket. Criminals know that phones contain banking apps, social media accounts, personal photos, and access to email systems that can be used to reset passwords for other accounts.

Modern smartphones are more secure than most people's computers, but only if you activate the security features and configure them properly. Most families use phones with default settings that prioritize convenience over protection, creating opportunities for criminals to exploit both lost devices and remote attacks.

iPhone Security: The Walled Garden Approach

Apple designed iOS with security as a fundamental feature rather than an optional add-on. The operating system includes strong encryption, app sandboxing, and automatic security updates that protect against most common threats.

Enable Face ID or Touch ID along with a strong passcode. Biometric authentication provides convenience for daily use while the passcode ensures you can access your phone even if the biometric sensors fail or criminals try to force you to unlock the device.

Choose a six-digit passcode instead of a four-digit code. The extra digits provide significantly more security against brute force attacks while still being easy to remember. Avoid using obvious patterns like 123456 or repeating digits like 111111.

Configure automatic iOS updates to install security patches as soon as Apple releases them. iOS updates include critical security fixes that protect against vulnerabilities that criminals actively exploit.

Enable "Erase Data" after ten failed passcode attempts. This setting automatically deletes all information on your phone if someone tries to guess your passcode repeatedly. The feature sounds extreme, but it prevents criminals from using automated tools to crack your passcode.

A family's phone was stolen during a vacation in Italy, but they'd enabled Find My iPhone and the device was still connected to wifi in the thief's apartment.

Instead of just reporting the theft to police, the family used the Find My iPhone feature to display a message on the lock screen offering a $200 reward for the phone's return, no questions asked. They also included their hotel phone number.

The thief called within six hours. He claimed he'd "found" the phone and wanted to return it for the reward. The family met him at a public location, paid the reward, and got their phone back with all their vacation photos intact.

The $200 reward was less than the cost of replacing the phone and recovering their accounts. More importantly, they avoided the weeks of hassle that come with stolen device recovery. Sometimes paying a small ransom is more practical than fighting the theft.

Android Security: Freedom with Responsibility

Android's open architecture provides more customization options than iOS but requires more attention to security configuration. Different Android manufacturers add their own security features and modify Google's base security settings.

Keep Android updated to the latest available version. Android security updates are released monthly, but many phone manufacturers are slow to distribute them. Check for updates manually if your phone doesn't receive them automatically.

Enable Google Play Protect to scan apps for malware automatically. This cloud-based security service checks apps when you install them and continues monitoring for suspicious behavior after installation.

Install apps only from the Google Play Store unless you have specific technical requirements for alternative app sources. Google's app review process isn't perfect, but it catches most malware before it reaches the official store.

> ◆ **Personal Experience:** I tested Android security by intentionally installing malware on a test phone to see how quickly Google Play Protect would detect it. The malware was discovered and quarantined within twelve hours, demonstrating that Google's cloud-based scanning can catch threats that traditional antivirus software misses.

Disable "Unknown Sources" in your security settings to prevent installation of apps from outside the Play Store. This setting is often enabled by malware or by people trying to install pirated apps, but it creates serious security risks.

Use Google's two-factor authentication for your Google account. This protection prevents criminals from accessing your account even if they steal your password. Enable backup codes and store them securely in case you lose access to your phone.

Screen Lock Security for Both Platforms

Use the strongest screen lock method available on your phone: Face ID, Touch ID, or a strong passcode. Avoid pattern locks, which are easy for observers to memorize and reproduce.

Set your phone to lock automatically after one minute of inactivity. Longer timeout periods create opportunities for criminals to access your phone if you leave it unattended briefly.

Disable Siri or Google Assistant access from the lock screen. These voice assistants can often access personal information, send messages, and make calls without requiring you to unlock your phone first.

> ★ **Pro Tip:** Test your phone's security settings by asking a family member to try accessing your information while the phone is locked. You might be surprised by how much they can see and do without your passcode.

Configure emergency bypass for family members' phone calls. This feature allows calls from designated contacts to ring through even when your phone is in Do Not Disturb mode, ensuring you don't miss genuine emergencies.

Hide sensitive notifications from the lock screen. Banking apps, email previews, and text message content shouldn't be visible to anyone who glances at your phone while it's locked.

Tablet Security for Family Use: Shared Devices, Separate Lives

Tablets present unique security challenges because they're often shared between family members but contain personal information from multiple users. A tablet might have mom's banking apps, dad's work email, and children's social media accounts all on the same device.

User Account Management

Create separate user profiles for each family member who uses shared tablets. Both iOS and Android support multiple user accounts that keep each person's apps, files, and settings completely separate.

Set up parental controls for children's tablet accounts. These controls can restrict app installation, limit screen time, filter web content, and prevent purchases without adult approval.

Configure automatic logout or account switching when the tablet hasn't been used for a set period. This prevents family members from accidentally accessing each other's accounts and information.

Use different passcodes or biometric authentication for different user accounts. Each family member should have their own way to access their account without knowing other users' authentication methods.

App Store Restrictions

Disable in-app purchases for children's accounts or require password authentication for all purchases. Children often don't understand that "free" games can generate real charges through in-app purchases for virtual items.

Review and approve app installations for children's accounts. Many apps that seem appropriate for children collect extensive personal information or contain inappropriate advertising.

Check app permissions before installation to understand what information each app can access. Camera access, location tracking, and contact list access should be limited to apps that genuinely need these capabilities.

Remove unused apps regularly to reduce the attack surface on shared tablets. Apps that aren't being used still receive updates and could potentially be compromised by security vulnerabilities.

Content and Privacy Controls

Enable content filtering appropriate for the youngest users of shared tablets. These filters can block inappropriate websites, restrict mature content in app stores, and prevent access to explicit material.

Configure location services carefully for shared tablets. Children's games don't need to know your family's location, and location tracking can reveal personal information about your family's routines.

Review photo and video sharing settings to prevent accidental privacy breaches. Children might not understand the implications of sharing family photos with apps or online services.

Set up automatic backups for tablets but ensure each user's data goes to their own cloud storage account. Family photos and personal documents shouldn't all be mixed together in shared backup systems.

> **▲ Caution:** Shared tablets often become repositories for the entire family's personal information. Be extra careful about what apps you install and what permissions you grant on devices used by multiple people.

App Store Safety: Navigating the Wild West of Mobile Apps

App stores contain millions of applications, most of which are legitimate and useful. But criminals have learned to disguise malware as popular apps, create fake versions of legitimate apps, and even compromise legitimate apps after they've been approved for distribution.

Identifying Legitimate Apps

Download apps only from official app stores: Apple's App Store for iOS devices and Google Play Store for Android devices. Third-party app stores have much weaker security controls and are common sources of malware.

Check app developer information before installing anything. Legitimate apps are usually published by established companies with verifiable contact information and professional websites.

Read app reviews carefully, but be skeptical of reviews that seem fake or overly positive. Criminals often create fake reviews to make malicious apps appear legitimate and popular.

Verify app permissions match the app's stated functionality. A flashlight app shouldn't need access to your contacts, camera, or location. Games shouldn't need permission to read your text messages.

Look for apps with millions of downloads and thousands of reviews. While popularity doesn't guarantee safety, well-established apps are less likely to be malicious than obscure apps with few users.

Recognizing Malicious Apps

Be suspicious of apps that request excessive permissions for their stated functionality. Malware often asks for broad permissions that allow it to access information and features unrelated to the app's apparent purpose.

Avoid apps that promise unrealistic benefits: free premium content, unlimited in-game currency, or miraculous health improvements. These apps often deliver malware instead of their promised features.

Watch for apps that mimic popular games or services but have slightly different names or icons. Criminals create fake versions of popular apps to trick users into downloading malware.

> ■ **Danger Zone:** Never "jailbreak" iOS devices or "root" Android devices to install unauthorized apps. These modifications disable important security features and make your phone vulnerable to malware that would normally be blocked.

Be wary of apps that require you to disable security settings or install additional software. Legitimate apps work within the standard app store security model and don't require you to compromise your device's protection.

App Update Security

Enable automatic updates for apps to ensure you receive security patches quickly. Many app vulnerabilities are discovered and fixed regularly, but the patches only protect you if you install them promptly.

Review app update descriptions to understand what changes are being made. Updates that add new permissions or significantly change app functionality deserve extra scrutiny.

Remove apps that are no longer updated by their developers. Abandoned apps won't receive security patches and become increasingly vulnerable to attack as new vulnerabilities are discovered.

Check your installed apps monthly and remove ones you no longer use. Every app on your device represents a potential security risk, and unused apps provide no benefit to offset that risk.

Children and App Safety

Teach children to ask permission before installing any new apps, even free ones. Children often don't understand the security implications of app permissions and can accidentally install malware.

Review children's app usage regularly and remove apps that collect unnecessary personal information or display inappropriate advertising.

Explain to children why they shouldn't share personal information within apps, even in games that seem harmless. Many children's apps collect data that can be used for identity theft or targeted advertising.

Set up family sharing or parental control features that require adult approval for all app installations and purchases. These controls help prevent children from accidentally installing malicious or inappropriate apps.

Mobile Payment and Banking Security: Your Wallet in Your Phone

Mobile payment systems like Apple Pay, Google Pay, and banking apps have made financial transactions more convenient than ever. They've also created new opportunities for criminals to steal money and financial information from mobile devices.

Mobile Payment Security

Use built-in payment systems (Apple Pay, Google Pay) instead of storing credit card information in individual shopping apps. These payment systems provide stronger security and don't share your actual credit card numbers with merchants.

Enable transaction notifications for all mobile payment systems. These alerts let you know immediately when your payment methods are used, allowing you to spot unauthorized transactions quickly.

Remove saved payment methods from apps you no longer use regularly. Old shopping apps with stored credit card information create unnecessary risks without providing ongoing value.

Use biometric authentication for all payment apps when available. Fingerprint and face recognition provide quick access for legitimate users while making it much harder for criminals to make unauthorized transactions.

Set up spending limits and transaction alerts through your bank and credit card companies. These safeguards can prevent large unauthorized charges even if criminals gain access to your payment apps.

Banking App Security

Download banking apps only from official app stores and verify that they're published by your actual bank. Criminals create fake banking apps that steal login credentials and account information.

Enable all available security features in banking apps: biometric login, transaction alerts, and automatic logout after inactivity. These features provide multiple layers of protection against unauthorized access.

Never use banking apps on public WiFi networks, even networks that appear secure. Use your phone's cellular connection or a VPN service when accessing financial accounts away from home.

Log out of banking apps completely when finished rather than just closing them. Many apps continue running in the background and remain accessible without re-authentication.

Review banking app permissions and disable any that aren't necessary for core functionality. Banking apps shouldn't need access to your camera, microphone, or contact list unless you're using specific features that require these capabilities.

Criminals had created a fake version of a major bank's app that looked identical to the real one. They distributed it through text message phishing campaigns that claimed the recipient's account had been compromised and they needed to download an "updated security app."

The fake app collected login credentials and immediately transmitted them to criminal servers. But the criminals were clever: they also logged the victim into the real banking app in the background, so the victim saw their actual account information and assumed everything was working normally.

The criminals waited two weeks before using the stolen credentials, giving victims time to forget about the fake app download. When they finally started draining accounts, victims had no idea how their banking information had been compromised.

The attack was discovered only when a security researcher noticed that the fake app was requesting permissions that the real banking app didn't need. Tens of thousands of people had downloaded the malicious app before it was identified and removed.

Lost Device Protection

Enable remote wipe capabilities for all devices that contain financial apps. Both iOS and Android can erase devices remotely if they're lost or stolen, preventing criminals from accessing your financial accounts.

Set up find-my-device services that can locate lost phones and tablets. These services can help you recover lost devices before criminals have time to access your financial information.

Contact your bank immediately if a device with banking apps is lost or stolen. Many banks can temporarily disable mobile access to your accounts while you recover or replace your device.

Change passwords for all financial accounts accessed through a lost device. Even if you wipe the device remotely, criminals might have already accessed your accounts before the wipe command took effect.

Review account activity carefully for several weeks after losing a device. Criminals sometimes use stolen financial information weeks or months after the initial theft, hoping you've forgotten about the security breach.

Family Financial Safety

Teach children about the real-world value of virtual purchases and in-app transactions. Many children don't understand that spending virtual currency in games costs real money from family bank accounts.

Set up purchase approval requirements for all family members' devices. These controls prevent unauthorized spending and give you visibility into what family members are buying through their devices.

Monitor family members' app installations and remove games or apps that encourage excessive spending. Many mobile games are designed to extract maximum revenue through psychological manipulation tactics.

Create separate Apple ID or Google accounts for children so their purchases don't have access to adult payment methods. Children's accounts can use gift cards or allowance credits instead of direct access to family bank accounts.

> ◆ **Personal Experience:** I helped a family whose eight-year-old had spent $1,400 on in-app purchases in a single weekend. The child was playing a "free" game that sold virtual gems for real money. Each purchase was small ($2-5), but the child made hundreds of purchases without understanding they were spending real money. The family eventually recovered most of the charges, but it took three months of disputes with the app store and game developer.

Mobile devices are your family's most personal computers, containing more intimate information than any other technology you own. They deserve the strongest security you can provide because the consequences of mobile device compromise extend far beyond the cost of replacing the hardware.

The convenience that makes mobile devices so useful also makes them attractive targets for criminals. Every app you install, every payment method you save, and every account you access creates new opportunities for criminals to steal your information and money.

But with proper security configuration and careful app management, mobile devices can be both convenient and secure. The key is treating your phone and tablet as the powerful computers they really are, not as simple communication devices that don't need security attention.

Chapter 7: Entertainment and Gaming - The Forgotten Risk

The Xbox that mysteriously ordered $200 worth of games

The Fletcher family woke up to an email confirming their *purchase of $247.83 worth of Xbox games and downloadable content. The problem was, nobody in the family had bought anything. Their credit card had been charged for games they'd never heard of, downloadable content for games they didn't own, and virtual currency for online games none of them played.*

The Xbox had been making purchases automatically throughout the night while the family slept. Someone had gained access to their Xbox Live account and was using their stored credit card information to buy games and virtual items. The purchases were small enough that the credit card company's fraud detection didn't trigger, but they added up to hundreds of dollars.

When they investigated, the Fletchers discovered their Xbox had been compromised for months. Criminals had been selling access to their account to other players who wanted free games and virtual currency. The family's entertainment system had become a criminal shopping mall where strangers bought digital goods with their money.

The worst part? The criminals had also been reading their private messages, monitoring their friends list, and tracking what games their children played. The Xbox contained detailed information about the family's schedules, preferences, and relationships that had been exposed to unknown criminals for months.

The Fletchers had spent thousands of dollars on security systems to protect their home from physical burglary, but they'd never considered that their entertainment devices needed the same level of protection. They assumed that game consoles were toys, not computers that could be hacked and exploited.

Your family's entertainment devices are powerful computers disguised as toys and appliances. They connect to the internet, store personal information, and provide access to financial accounts. Yet most families secure them like furniture instead of like the sophisticated networked computers they really are.

Smart TV Security and Privacy: When Your TV Watches You Back

Smart TVs collect more personal information about your family than any other device in your home. They know what shows you watch, when you watch them, how long you watch, and what advertisements capture your attention. This information creates detailed profiles of your family's habits, preferences, and routines.

The Data Collection Reality

Smart TVs use Automatic Content Recognition (ACR) to identify everything displayed on your screen: broadcast television, streaming services, gaming content, and even content from connected devices like laptops and phones. This technology creates detailed logs of your family's viewing habits that get sold to advertisers and data brokers.

Your TV records not just what you watch, but how you watch it. Do you fast-forward through commercials? Do you pause during dramatic scenes? Do you change channels when certain types of content appear? All of this behavioral data gets analyzed and used to build psychological profiles for targeted advertising.

Many smart TVs contain microphones that listen for voice commands, but these microphones can also record background conversations when the TV appears to be off. The microphones are designed to activate when they hear specific wake words, but they sometimes misinterpret normal conversation as activation commands.

The Rahman family discovered their TV's listening capabilities when they received targeted advertisements for medical treatments they'd never searched for online. Their smart TV had recorded a private conversation about their daughter's learning disability and shared this information with advertising companies that used it to target relevant ads.

Privacy Settings Configuration

Disable ACR and automatic content recognition features in your TV's privacy settings. These features are usually enabled by default and buried deep in settings menus where most people never find them.

Turn off voice recognition and wake word detection unless you actively use voice commands to control your TV. These features create privacy risks without providing significant convenience benefits for most families.

Disable sharing of viewing data with third-party companies. Most smart TVs allow you to opt out of data sharing, but the settings are often confusing and may require you to decline multiple different types of data collection.

Review and delete stored voice recordings regularly. Many smart TVs keep recordings of voice commands and background audio that can be accessed through manufacturer websites or companion apps.

Configure guest mode settings to prevent visitors from accidentally accessing your family's viewing profiles or sharing their viewing habits with your accounts.

> ★ **Pro Tip:** Create a separate network specifically for smart TVs and entertainment devices. This isolation prevents compromised entertainment devices from accessing your family's computers and phones.

Manufacturer Account Security

Smart TVs often require accounts with manufacturers like Samsung, LG, or Sony to access streaming apps and advanced features. These accounts store personal information and viewing preferences that need protection.

Use strong, unique passwords for all smart TV manufacturer accounts. These passwords should be different from any other accounts you use and generated by a password manager.

Enable two-factor authentication on manufacturer accounts when available. This extra security prevents criminals from accessing your account even if they steal your password.

Review connected apps and services regularly. Smart TVs can connect to social media accounts, email services, and cloud storage that might expose additional personal information.

Remove stored payment information from smart TV accounts unless you regularly purchase content through the TV interface. Stored credit card information creates opportunities for unauthorized purchases.

> ◆ **Personal Experience:** I helped a family whose smart TV was infected with malware that turned the device into a cryptocurrency mining operation. The TV's processor was being used to generate digital currency for criminals while driving up the family's electricity bill. The infection was so sophisticated that the TV continued working normally for entertainment while secretly performing calculations in the background.

Gaming Console Account Protection: Securing Your Digital Playground

Gaming consoles store vast amounts of personal information: credit card details for digital purchases, friends lists with real names and contact information, voice and text communications, and detailed gaming patterns that reveal personal schedules and preferences.

PlayStation and Xbox Account Security

Console accounts are valuable targets because they often contain stored payment methods and provide access to social networks of gamers who trust each other. Criminals can use compromised accounts to make unauthorized purchases, steal personal information, and launch social engineering attacks against friends and family.

Enable two-factor authentication on all gaming console accounts. PlayStation, Xbox, and Nintendo all support additional authentication methods that prevent unauthorized access even if criminals steal your password.

Review payment methods stored in console accounts and remove any that aren't actively needed. Consider using prepaid gaming cards instead of credit cards for digital purchases to limit potential losses from account compromises.

Set up spending limits and purchase notifications through your console's parental controls or account settings. These safeguards prevent large unauthorized charges and alert you immediately when purchases are made.

Configure privacy settings to limit who can see your gaming activity, friends list, and personal information. Default privacy settings often share more information than necessary with other players and gaming services.

Change console account passwords immediately if you notice any suspicious activity: unexpected purchases, messages you didn't send, or friends added without your permission.

Children's Gaming Account Management

Children's gaming accounts need extra protection because young players often don't understand the security implications of sharing personal information or the real-world value of virtual purchases.

Create separate child accounts with restricted permissions rather than letting children use adult accounts. Child accounts can have spending limits, communication restrictions, and content filters that adult accounts typically don't include.

Review and approve friend requests for children's gaming accounts. Many online predators use gaming platforms to identify and communicate with potential victims through friend requests and private messages.

Monitor in-game purchases and virtual currency transactions. Many "free" games generate revenue through psychological manipulation that encourages excessive spending on virtual items.

Teach children about the permanence of online communications and the importance of reporting inappropriate behavior from other players. Gaming platforms often include reporting mechanisms for harassment, bullying, and inappropriate content.

A twelve-year-old discovered he could buy virtual currency in his favorite mobile game using his mother's credit card, which was stored in the family iPad for "emergency purchases."

The child didn't understand that the virtual gems cost real money. Each purchase was small ($1.99 to $4.99), but he made dozens of purchases every day for two weeks. By the time his *mother noticed, he'd spent $2,847 on virtual items in a single mobile game.*

The game's design encouraged frequent small purchases through psychological manipulation: artificial scarcity, time-limited offers, and social pressure to keep up with other players. The child thought he was just playing a game, but he was being systematically exploited by predatory business practices.

The family eventually recovered most of the money through credit card disputes, but it took six months of fighting with the game developer and app store. The child learned an expensive lesson about the difference between virtual currency and real money.

Gaming Communication Safety

Gaming platforms include text chat, voice chat, and video communication features that create opportunities for criminals to contact and manipulate players, especially children.

Disable voice chat for children's accounts or restrict it to friends only. Many gaming platforms allow anyone to initiate voice conversations with players, creating opportunities for inappropriate contact.

Review text chat logs periodically to identify potential grooming attempts or cyberbullying. Many gaming platforms store chat histories that parents can access through account management interfaces.

Report suspicious behavior immediately through gaming platform reporting systems. Platform operators take reports of predatory behavior seriously and can ban problematic users from their services.

Teach children to never share personal information through gaming platforms: real names, addresses, school information, or family details should never be discussed with online gaming contacts.

Configure streaming and broadcast settings to prevent children from accidentally sharing personal information when streaming their gameplay to public audiences.

Streaming Device Security: Protecting Your Entertainment Gateway

Streaming devices like Roku, Apple TV, Amazon Fire TV, and Chromecast are specialized computers that connect your television to internet content. They store account credentials for multiple streaming services and often have access to personal information from connected phones and tablets.

Account Management for Streaming Services

Streaming devices store login credentials for dozens of services: Netflix, Amazon Prime, Disney+, HBO Max, and many others. These stored credentials create opportunities for criminals to access your entertainment accounts and the personal information they contain.

Use different passwords for each streaming service account. Many families use the same password for multiple entertainment accounts, creating opportunities for criminals to access multiple services after compromising a single account.

Enable two-factor authentication on streaming service accounts that support it. Netflix, Amazon Prime, and Disney+ all offer additional security features that prevent unauthorized access.

Review active device lists in streaming service account settings. These lists show which devices are currently logged into your accounts and can help you identify unauthorized access.

Remove streaming devices from your accounts before selling, donating, or disposing of them. Many families forget to log out of streaming services when replacing old devices, leaving their accounts accessible to the devices' new owners.

Log out of streaming services when staying in hotels or using temporary accommodations. Hotel TVs and rental property devices might retain your login credentials and provide access to future guests.

Device-Specific Security Settings

Configure automatic software updates for all streaming devices. These devices receive security patches regularly, but many require manual intervention to install updates.

Disable features you don't use: voice control, mobile app connectivity, and automatic content recommendations. Each enabled feature creates additional attack surfaces that criminals can potentially exploit.

Review privacy settings for streaming devices and disable data sharing with third-party companies when possible. Many streaming devices collect viewing habits and sell this information to advertisers.

Set up PIN codes for purchases and account changes on streaming devices. These codes prevent unauthorized purchases and account modifications if someone gains temporary access to your devices.

Use guest modes or restricted profiles for visitors and children. These limited access modes prevent temporary users from accessing your full account information or making unwanted changes to your settings.

> ▲ **Caution:** Many streaming devices continue collecting data and monitoring usage even when they appear to be turned off. They're often in standby mode rather than completely powered down, maintaining network connections that can be exploited by attackers.

Children's Gaming Safety: Protecting Young Players

Online gaming exposes children to risks that don't exist in traditional offline play: contact with strangers, exposure to inappropriate content, cyberbullying, predatory behavior, and psychological manipulation designed to extract money.

Age-Appropriate Gaming Controls

Research game content ratings before allowing children to play new games. The Entertainment Software Rating Board (ESRB) provides detailed information about violence, language, sexual content, and other potentially inappropriate material.

Use parental control features built into gaming consoles and gaming services. These controls can restrict game purchases, limit communication with other players, and filter inappropriate content.

Set time limits for gaming sessions to prevent excessive play that interferes with sleep, schoolwork, and family activities. Many gaming platforms include built-in time management features.

Create separate gaming spaces in public areas of your home where you can monitor children's gaming activities and interactions with other players.

Review children's friend lists regularly and investigate any adult contacts or players with inappropriate usernames or profile information.

Online Interaction Management

Teach children to recognize and report inappropriate behavior from other players: requests for personal information, attempts to move conversations off the gaming platform, or discussions of topics that make them uncomfortable.

Explain the difference between gaming friends and real-world friends. Online gaming relationships should remain within the gaming environment and not extend to other forms of communication.

Monitor children's spending on virtual items and explain the real-world cost of in-game purchases. Many children don't understand that virtual currency represents real money from family bank accounts.

Set up approval processes for new game installations and friend requests. Children should ask permission before downloading new games or accepting contact from unknown players.

Create family rules about gaming communication: no sharing personal information, no meeting online friends in person, and immediate reporting of any concerning interactions.

Predator Awareness and Prevention

Online gaming platforms are common hunting grounds for predators who use games to identify and groom potential victims. These criminals understand gaming culture and use it to build trust with children.

Watch for warning signs of inappropriate contact: secretive behavior about gaming activities, reluctance to discuss online friends, or attempts to use gaming devices privately without supervision.

Teach children about gradual boundary crossing: how predators slowly introduce inappropriate topics and requests for personal information over time.

Explain why real-world meetings with online gaming contacts are dangerous and should never be attempted without extensive parental supervision and verification.

Create open communication channels where children feel safe reporting concerning interactions without fear of losing gaming privileges.

> ■ **Danger Zone:** Gaming platforms that allow user-generated content (custom maps, player-created avatars, text chat) have weaker content moderation and higher risks of exposing children to inappropriate material and predatory behavior.

Family Gaming Policies

Establish clear rules about gaming time, appropriate games, and acceptable online behavior. These policies should be discussed with children and consistently enforced by all family members.

Create consequences for violating gaming safety rules that are educational rather than purely punitive. Help children understand why certain behaviors are dangerous rather than just forbidding them.

Schedule regular family discussions about online gaming experiences, both positive and negative. These conversations help children process their online interactions and identify potential problems.

Stay informed about gaming trends, popular games, and emerging risks in gaming communities. Gaming culture evolves rapidly, and new risks emerge as technology and player behavior change.

Consider playing games with your children to better understand their gaming experiences and the communities they're participating in.

Entertainment devices represent some of the most overlooked security risks in modern homes. Families invest thousands of dollars in sophisticated security systems to protect their physical property while leaving entertainment devices completely unprotected despite the valuable personal information they contain.

The convenience and enjoyment these devices provide shouldn't come at the cost of your family's privacy and security. With proper configuration and ongoing monitoring, entertainment devices can provide safe, secure entertainment that doesn't expose your family to unnecessary risks.

But remember that entertainment device security is just one component of your household's overall protection plan. The information and access these devices provide to criminals can be used to compromise other aspects of your connected life, making entertainment security a critical foundation for protecting everything else.

PART IV: Managing your Digital Life

Chapter 8: Passwords and Access - Doing It Right Without Going Crazy

Noah's birthday password and how thieves emptied his bank account

Noah Brennan used the same password for everything: his birth date followed by his first name. 08151985Noah was easy to remember and met the basic requirements for most websites. It worked for his email, his bank account, his work computer, and dozens of online shopping sites.

The password seemed secure to Noah because it was personal and meaningful. Only he knew his birthday and name, right? Wrong. Criminals gathered this information from social media profiles, public records, and data breaches in minutes. His birthday was listed on his Facebook profile. His full name appeared in voter registration records. His address and phone number were available through online directories.

When criminals compromised a gaming website that stored passwords in plain text, they gained access to Noah's email account because he'd used the same password for both. From his email, they reset passwords for his bank account, credit cards, and investment accounts. They transferred $12,000 from his checking account, opened three new credit cards, and applied for a personal loan using his identity.

The attack succeeded in one weekend because Noah had made password security too simple. His easy-to-remember password was also easy for criminals to guess. His convenient approach to password management gave criminals convenient access to his entire financial life.

Noah's story isn't unusual. Most families use password strategies that prioritize convenience over security, creating opportunities for criminals to compromise multiple accounts after stealing a single password.

The Password Reality Check: Why Everything You've Been Told Is Wrong

Traditional password advice has failed miserably. Security experts told people to create complex passwords with numbers, symbols, and mixed capitalization. They said to change passwords every 90 days and never write them down. The result was passwords that humans couldn't remember but computers could crack in hours.

People responded by creating passwords that met the technical requirements but were predictable and weak: Password1!, Summer2024!, or Company123!. These passwords look complex but follow patterns that password-cracking software recognizes easily.

The complexity requirements made password management so difficult that people started reusing passwords across multiple accounts. A single data breach could suddenly expose dozens of accounts because everyone used the same "complex" password everywhere.

Password expiration policies made the problem worse. People changed their passwords by adding numbers or incrementing dates: Password1! became Password2!, then Password3!. These predictable changes provided no real security improvement while making password management more frustrating.

◆ **Personal Experience:** I tested password strength by trying to crack passwords from a voluntary security assessment. Complex passwords like "P@ssword!" took my software 23 minutes to crack, while simple passphrases like "coffee table lamp shade" took over 900 years. Length matters more than complexity, but most password policies focus on complexity at the expense of length.

Modern password security focuses on three principles: length, uniqueness, and protection. Long passwords are exponentially harder to crack than complex short passwords. Unique passwords prevent single breaches from compromising multiple accounts. Protected passwords stored in password managers eliminate the memory burden that causes people to make poor security choices.

Password Managers for Families: Your Digital Keychain

Password managers solve the fundamental problem of password security: the conflict between security and usability. They generate strong, unique passwords for every account and remember them so you don't have to.

Choosing a Family Password Manager

Select a password manager that supports family sharing and multiple user accounts. Services like 1Password, Bitwarden, and Dashlane offer family plans that let you share some passwords while keeping others private.

Look for password managers that work across all the devices your family uses: Windows computers, Macs, iPhones, Android phones, and tablets. The password manager should sync automatically between devices so passwords are available wherever you need them.

Choose services that offer emergency access features. These features let designated family members access your passwords if something happens to you, ensuring that important accounts don't become inaccessible during emergencies.

Evaluate the user interface and setup complexity. Family members with different technical skill levels need to be able to use the password manager successfully, or they'll create workarounds that defeat the security benefits.

Consider the total cost for your family size and compare it to the potential cost of identity theft recovery. Password manager family plans typically cost $3-8 per month, which is far less than the average cost of recovering from password-related security breaches.

Setting Up Family Password Sharing

Create separate vaults or collections for different types of shared passwords: streaming services that the whole family uses, home security systems that adults need to manage, and emergency contacts that everyone should be able to access.

Keep individual banking and personal accounts in private vaults that only you can access. Children don't need passwords for their parents' financial accounts, and teenagers don't need access to sensitive family business information.

Set up shared folders for accounts that multiple family members need: WiFi passwords, streaming services, gaming accounts, and cloud storage. These shared folders eliminate the need to text passwords between family members.

Configure different permission levels for family members based on their age and responsibility level. Younger children might have read-only access to shared passwords, while teenagers could have full access to entertainment accounts but restricted access to financial services.

Train all family members on how to use the password manager before requiring them to use it for important accounts. People who don't understand how password managers work will create insecure workarounds that defeat the purpose.

A father installed a family password manager but his teenage daughter refused to use it because she was "too busy to learn new software." She continued using the same password for everything and writing it on sticky notes.

The father solved the problem by changing the WiFi password to a 32-character random string generated by the password manager. The WiFi password was only available through the family's password manager app. Within three days, his daughter had learned to use the password manager because it was the only way to get online.

The approach was sneaky but effective. Instead of arguing about password security in abstract terms, he created a practical situation where the password manager was the easiest solution to an immediate problem. Once his daughter understood how convenient password managers could be, she started using it for all her accounts voluntarily.

Password Manager Security Features

Enable two-factor authentication for your password manager account. This extra security layer protects the system that protects all your other passwords. Use an authenticator app rather than text message codes for the strongest protection.

Configure secure password sharing that doesn't expose passwords in plain text. Good password managers let you share account access without revealing the actual passwords to other family members.

Use the password manager's security audit features to identify weak, reused, or compromised passwords. These audits help you prioritize which passwords need to be updated first and identify accounts that might have been exposed in data breaches.

Set up automatic password changing for supported websites. Some password managers can automatically update passwords for popular services, reducing the maintenance burden of keeping passwords secure.

Enable breach monitoring that alerts you when your email addresses or passwords appear in new data breaches. This early warning system helps you respond quickly to potential account compromises.

> ★ **Pro Tip:** Start using a password manager for new accounts only. Don't try to migrate all existing passwords at once. As you log into existing accounts, let the password manager generate new strong passwords and store them. This gradual approach prevents the overwhelming feeling that stops many people from adopting password managers.

Two-Factor Authentication Setup: Your Account's Security Guard

Two-factor authentication (2FA) requires something you know (your password) plus something you have (your phone or a security key) to access your accounts. This second layer of security prevents most account compromises even when criminals steal your passwords.

Understanding Authentication Methods

Text message codes are the most common form of 2FA, but they're also the weakest. Criminals can intercept text messages, clone phone numbers, or trick phone companies into transferring your number to their devices.

Authenticator apps like Google Authenticator, Microsoft Authenticator, or Authy generate time-based codes that change every 30 seconds. These apps work even when your phone doesn't have internet access and are much more secure than text message codes.

Hardware security keys like YubiKey or Google Titan provide the strongest 2FA protection. These physical devices must be plugged into your computer or held near your phone to complete login. Criminals can't compromise hardware keys remotely.

Push notifications from apps like Microsoft Authenticator or Duo send approval requests to your phone when someone tries to log into your accounts. You can approve legitimate login attempts and deny unauthorized access attempts with a single tap.

Backup codes are one-time-use passwords that let you access your accounts if you lose your phone or security key. Store these codes securely and separately from the devices they're meant to replace.

Prioritizing 2FA Implementation

Enable 2FA on your most critical accounts first: email, banking, cloud storage, and password manager accounts. On most services, the setting lives under Account Settings, then Security or Privacy — look for "Two-Step Verification," "Two-Factor Authentication," or "Login Security." The label varies but the function is the same.

Set up 2FA for social media accounts that contain personal information or could be used to impersonate you. Criminals often use compromised social media accounts to scam friends and family members.

Protect work accounts that could expose your employer's systems or provide access to sensitive business information. Many workplace security breaches start with compromised employee personal accounts.

Configure 2FA for gaming and entertainment accounts that store payment information. These accounts might seem less critical, but they often contain credit card details and can be used for unauthorized purchases.

Consider the convenience versus security trade-off for each account. Critical financial accounts deserve the strongest 2FA methods even if they're less convenient, while entertainment accounts might use simpler methods that balance security with usability.

Family 2FA Management

Set up 2FA methods that work for each family member's technical comfort level. Teenagers might be comfortable with authenticator apps, while elderly relatives might prefer text message codes despite their security limitations.

Create backup authentication methods for shared family accounts. If the primary 2FA device is lost or broken, backup methods prevent the entire family from losing access to important accounts.

Train family members to recognize and respond to unexpected 2FA requests. Criminals sometimes try to trigger 2FA codes to trick people into providing access to their accounts.

> ▲ **Caution:** Never share 2FA codes with anyone, even family members or people claiming to be from the services you use. Legitimate companies will never ask you to provide 2FA codes over the phone or through email.

Document 2FA backup codes and store them securely where multiple family members can access them during emergencies. These codes should be treated like important financial documents.

Plan for device replacement scenarios where 2FA apps need to be transferred to new phones. Many people lock themselves out of accounts when they get new phones because they forget to transfer their authenticator apps.

Secure Account Sharing: When Families Need Common Access

Some accounts naturally need to be shared between family members: streaming services, cloud storage, home security systems, and shared email accounts. Secure sharing requires careful planning to provide access without compromising security.

Shared Account Strategy

Create dedicated accounts for services that multiple family members need to use instead of sharing personal accounts. A family Netflix account is better than everyone using mom's personal Netflix login.

Use different access levels when services support them. Google Drive, for example, lets you share folders with view-only, comment, or edit permissions depending on what each family member needs to do.

Set up separate user profiles within shared accounts when possible. Many streaming services, gaming platforms, and cloud storage services support multiple user profiles that keep individual preferences and activity separate.

Configure activity monitoring for shared accounts so you can identify unauthorized access or inappropriate usage. Most services provide activity logs that show when accounts were accessed and what actions were performed.

Establish family rules about shared account usage: what content is appropriate, spending limits for accounts with payment methods, and consequences for misusing shared access.

Temporary Access Management

Create guest accounts or temporary access methods for visitors, babysitters, and household workers who need limited access to your systems. Many smart home systems and streaming services support guest modes with restricted capabilities.

Use time-limited sharing for accounts that visitors might need temporarily. Some password managers can create sharing links that expire automatically after a set period.

Remove temporary access immediately when it's no longer needed. Don't rely on memory to revoke access later; do it immediately when temporary users leave your home.

Monitor shared accounts more frequently when temporary users have had access. Check activity logs and account settings to ensure temporary users didn't make unauthorized changes.

Change passwords for shared accounts periodically, especially if temporary users have had access or if you suspect unauthorized usage.

Family Account Security Policies

Establish clear rules about which family members can access which types of shared accounts. Financial accounts should generally not be shared with children, while entertainment accounts might be accessible to the whole family.

Create approval processes for adding new shared accounts or changing existing account settings. Children shouldn't be able to add new streaming services or modify parental controls without adult permission.

Set up spending notifications and limits for shared accounts that include payment methods. These controls prevent unauthorized purchases and help you monitor how shared accounts are being used.

Document shared account credentials in your family password manager with clear notes about who should have access and what the account is used for.

Review shared account access quarterly and remove family members who no longer need access or who have moved out of the household.

> ■ **Danger Zone:** Never share passwords by writing them down, sending them through text messages, or saying them out loud where others can overhear. Use secure sharing features in password managers or create temporary access methods instead.

Teaching Password Security to Family Members

Different family members need different approaches to password security education. Children need to understand basic concepts, teenagers need to learn about social engineering threats, and adults need practical skills for managing complex password requirements.

Age-Appropriate Password Education

Teach young children that passwords are like house keys: they protect important things and should never be shared with strangers. Use physical analogies that children can understand and relate to their existing knowledge about security.

Explain to teenagers how criminals use social engineering to trick people into revealing passwords. Show them examples of phishing emails, fake websites, and social media scams that target their age group.

Help adults understand the economics of cybercrime and why criminals target regular families. Many adults don't realize that their personal information has significant value to criminals.

Use real-world examples and current events to illustrate password security concepts. Data breaches, celebrity account hacks, and local cybercrime news help make abstract security concepts concrete and relevant.

Practice password security scenarios with family members: what to do if they suspect their password has been compromised, how to recognize phishing attempts, and when to ask for help with security decisions.

Building Security Habits

Start with small, manageable changes rather than trying to implement perfect security immediately. Begin with password managers for new accounts, then gradually migrate existing accounts to stronger passwords.

Celebrate security successes when family members make good password choices or identify potential threats. Positive reinforcement works better than criticism for building long-term security habits.

Make password security a regular family discussion topic, not a one-time lecture. Technology and threats change constantly, so security education needs to be ongoing.

Provide technical support when family members struggle with password managers or 2FA setup. Don't assume that everyone finds technology as easy to use as you do.

Lead by example with your own password security practices. Family members are more likely to adopt secure habits when they see other family members using them successfully.

Common Password Mistakes to Address

Explain why writing passwords on sticky notes defeats the purpose of having passwords. Help family members understand secure alternatives like password managers.

Address the temptation to use the same password for multiple accounts. Show family members how to use password managers to make unique passwords just as convenient as reused passwords.

Teach family members to recognize password reset scams that try to trick people into changing their passwords through fake emails or phone calls.

Help family members understand why "security questions" are often insecure and how to create answers that can't be guessed from social media or public records.

Demonstrate how criminals crack common password patterns and why seemingly clever passwords like "P@ssword!" are weak and predictable.

Password security doesn't have to be complicated or inconvenient. Modern tools like password managers and two-factor authentication make strong security easier than weak security once you understand how to use them properly.

The investment in setting up proper password management pays dividends immediately through reduced stress about account security and long-term protection against the growing threat of cybercrime targeting families.

But remember that passwords are just one layer of your family's security strategy. Strong passwords protect your accounts, but they can't protect against all the other ways criminals might try to compromise your family's digital life.

Chapter 9: Backing Up What Matters - Your Digital Insurance Policy

My 300,000 photos and the 10-minute windows when the dying drive worked

The hard drive started making clicking sounds on a Tuesday morning while I was editing photos from my latest wedding shoot. By Wednesday, the clicks had become grinding noises that sounded like a coffee grinder full of gravel. By Thursday, the drive would only work for ten minutes at a time before overheating and shutting down.

I had 300,000 photos on that drive. Twenty years of professional photography work. Wedding albums, family portraits, landscapes from national parks, and personal photos of my own family's milestones. The drive contained my entire career and most of my personal memories, all stored in one place with no backup.

For the next three weeks, I nursed that dying drive back to life ten minutes at a time. I'd turn it on, copy as many files as possible before it overheated, then wait an hour for it to cool down enough to try again. Each ten-minute window felt like performing surgery while the patient flatlined repeatedly.

I managed to recover about 85% of the photos, but the experience taught me a brutal lesson about the difference between thinking you have backups and having backups. I thought I was being careful by storing everything on a "reliable" external drive. I learned that any single storage device is just a mechanical failure away from catastrophe.

The photos I lost included some of my best work and irreplaceable family memories. But the worst part was realizing how easily preventable the disaster had been. A simple backup strategy would have protected everything, but

Your family probably makes the same mistake I made. You store important files carefully, but you don't protect them against the inevitable failure of the devices that contain them.

The Backup Reality: Everything Fails Eventually

Every storage device will fail. Hard drives have moving parts that wear out. Solid-state drives have limited write cycles that eventually exhaust. Cloud storage services go out of business or lose data. The question isn't whether your storage will fail, but when and whether you'll be prepared.

Most families have what I call "fake backups": copies of files stored on the same device, files moved between devices without keeping originals, or cloud storage that syncs corrupted files across all devices. These approaches give you the feeling of protection without actual protection.

Real backups follow the 3-2-1 rule: three copies of important data, stored on two different types of media, with one copy kept offsite. This rule protects against device failures, disasters that destroy your home, and mistakes that corrupt multiple copies simultaneously.

◆ **Personal Experience:** I helped a family recover from a house fire that destroyed their computers, external drives, and backup disks stored in the same home office. Their only surviving photos were low-resolution copies automatically uploaded to social media. They learned that having multiple backups in one location provides no protection against disasters that affect the entire location.

The biggest barrier to effective backup isn't technical complexity; it's the psychological difficulty of planning for disasters you haven't experienced yet. People who've never lost important data have trouble motivating themselves to invest time and money in backup systems that seem like unnecessary insurance.

But families who have experienced data loss become backup evangelists overnight. Nothing motivates proper backup planning like watching years of family photos disappear forever.

Understanding What You're Really Protecting

Your family's digital assets have value far beyond their storage cost. Family photos capture memories that can't be recreated. Financial documents provide proof of important transactions. Personal documents establish identity and legal relationships.

Calculate the replacement cost of your family's digital information. How much would you pay to recover lost photos, recreate financial records, or restore years of family videos? The emotional value often exceeds any realistic monetary calculation.

Consider the time investment represented by your digital files. Years of family photos, carefully organized documents, and accumulated digital possessions represent hundreds of hours of work that would be impossible to recreate.

Think about the legal and practical implications of losing important documents. Tax records, insurance policies, medical records, and legal documents might be required for future transactions or disputes.

Family Cloud Storage Strategies: Building Your Digital Safety Net

Cloud storage has revolutionized backup by making offsite storage accessible and affordable for families. But cloud storage also introduces new risks and requires careful planning to provide real protection rather than false security.

Choosing Family Cloud Storage Services

Select cloud storage providers with strong security reputations and financial stability. Companies like Google, Microsoft, Apple, and Dropbox have the resources to maintain reliable services and defend against attacks.

Evaluate storage capacity requirements for your entire family's current and future needs. Start with more capacity than you think you need because data storage requirements grow faster than most people expect.

Consider the integration between cloud storage and your family's devices. Services that work smoothly with your phones, tablets, and computers are more likely to be used consistently.

Research the provider's data recovery policies and disaster protection measures. Where do they store backups of your data? How quickly can they restore access if their systems fail?

Compare family sharing features that let multiple family members access shared folders while maintaining private storage areas. Look for granular permission controls that let you share some files while keeping others private.

A family had been faithfully backing up to a cloud storage service for three years, religiously checking that their files were uploading successfully. When their computer crashed, they discovered that the cloud service had been synchronizing empty placeholder files instead of their actual photos and documents.

The cloud service's software had a bug that created zero-byte files with correct names but no content. The family's backup monitoring showed successful uploads because the files were technically being synchronized, but the actual data was never leaving their computer.

The bug affected thousands of customers for over a year before it was discovered and fixed. The families affected lost data not because the cloud service was unreliable, but because they hadn't tested their backups to verify that the uploaded files contained their data.

The incident taught me that successful backup requires not just uploading files, but periodically downloading and verifying that the backed-up data is recoverable.

Cloud Storage Security Configuration

Enable two-factor authentication for all cloud storage accounts. These accounts often contain your family's most sensitive information and deserve the strongest protection available.

Configure sharing permissions carefully to prevent accidental exposure of private files. Default sharing settings often make files more accessible than necessary for your family's needs.

Use client-side encryption for particularly sensitive files before uploading them to cloud storage. This extra layer of protection ensures that even your cloud storage provider can't access your most private information.

Review account activity logs regularly to identify unauthorized access or suspicious activity. Most cloud storage providers offer detailed logs of who accessed your files and when.

Set up alerts for unusual activity: large downloads, access from new devices, or changes to important files. These notifications help you detect potential compromises quickly.

Family Cloud Storage Organization

Create a logical folder structure that all family members can understand and follow. Consistent organization makes it easier to find files and ensures that backups include everything important.

Establish naming conventions for files and folders that prevent confusion and duplication. Clear naming helps family members find files quickly and reduces the risk of accidentally deleting important information.

Set up automatic synchronization for important folders while being selective about what gets backed up. Not everything on your devices needs to be stored in the cloud, and storage costs can add up quickly.

Configure version history settings to keep multiple versions of important files. This protection helps you recover from accidental changes or corruption that might not be noticed immediately.

Use shared folders for information that multiple family members need to access while maintaining private folders for personal files.

★ **Pro Tip:** Create a "Family Archive" folder in your cloud storage that contains scanned copies of important physical documents: birth certificates, passports, insurance policies, and other papers that would be difficult to replace if lost.

Automatic Backup Across Devices: Set It and Forget It

The best backup system is one that works automatically without requiring daily attention or maintenance. Manual backup systems fail because people forget to use them consistently, especially when nothing has gone wrong recently.

Device-Specific Backup Solutions

Configure automatic backup on every device your family uses. iPhones can back up to iCloud automatically, Android phones can sync to Google Drive, and computers can use built-in backup systems like Time Machine or File History.

Enable photo backup from all family devices to prevent the loss of irreplaceable memories. Modern phones take thousands of photos per year, and losing these captures of daily life can be devastating.

Set up automatic document backup for work files and important personal documents. Configure backup software to monitor specific folders and upload changes automatically.

Use incremental backup systems that only copy changed files to reduce bandwidth usage and backup time. These systems make frequent backups practical even with large amounts of data.

Schedule automatic backups during times when devices aren't heavily used. Nighttime backup schedules ensure that backup operations don't interfere with daily device usage.

Cross-Platform Backup Strategies

Design backup systems that work across different types of devices and operating systems. Your family probably uses a mix of Windows computers, Macs, iPhones, and Android devices that need coordinated backup strategies.

Choose backup solutions that support all the file types your family creates: photos, videos, documents, music, and app data. Specialized file types might require specific backup approaches.

Plan for device replacement scenarios where backup systems need to restore data to new devices. Test the restoration process before you need it for a real emergency.

Consider bandwidth limitations and data caps when designing automatic backup systems. Large backup operations can interfere with other internet activities or exceed monthly data allowances.

Configure backup retention policies that keep multiple versions of files for different time periods. Recent files might need daily backups, while older files might only need monthly archival.

Monitoring Backup Success

Set up notifications that confirm when backups complete successfully and alert you when backups fail. Many backup systems fail silently, leaving families unprotected without realizing it.

Check backup logs regularly to ensure that all important files are being included in backup operations. New files and folders might not be included automatically if backup configurations aren't updated.

Test backup systems periodically by restoring small amounts of data to verify that the backup process is working correctly. Regular testing identifies problems before you need to rely on backups for real disasters.

Monitor storage usage in backup systems to ensure that you have adequate capacity for growing data needs. Backup systems that run out of space stop protecting new files without obvious warnings.

Document backup procedures and access information so that other family members can manage backup systems if needed.

> ▲ **Caution:** Automatic backup systems can propagate problems as well as protect against them. If malware encrypts your files, automatic backup might back up the encrypted versions and overwrite your good backups.

Backblaze: The Gold Standard for Family Backup

Backblaze Personal Backup stands out as one of the best backup solutions for families. For $60 per year per computer, Backblaze backs up everything on your computer to secure cloud storage with no storage limits.

Why Backblaze Works for Families

Backblaze eliminates the complexity that stops most families from implementing proper backup. Install the software, and it backs up everything on your computer automatically without requiring you to choose files or configure complex settings.

The unlimited storage model removes the anxiety about backup costs that prevent families from protecting large photo and video collections. You can back up terabytes of family memories without worrying about exceeding storage limits or facing surprise bills.

Backblaze runs continuously in the background, backing up new and changed files automatically. You don't need to remember to start backups or worry about whether important files are protected.

The service keeps multiple versions of files for 30 days (or longer with paid upgrades). This version history helps you recover from accidental changes or file corruption that might not be noticed immediately.

> ◆ **Personal Experience:** I've used Backblaze to recover from several disasters in the past decade. When my laptop was stolen from my car, I had a replacement computer up and running with all my files within 24 hours. When ransomware encrypted a client's computer, we restored everything from Backblaze and lost only four hours of work instead of years of business data.

Backblaze Security Features

Backblaze encrypts all data during transmission and storage using strong encryption that even Backblaze employees can't decrypt if you choose to manage your own encryption key.

You can set a private encryption key that only you know, ensuring that even if Backblaze's servers were compromised, your data would remain protected. This option provides maximum security while maintaining the convenience of cloud backup.

The service includes two-factor authentication to protect your account from unauthorized access. Even if criminals steal your Backblaze password, they can't access your backed-up data without your phone or authentication app.

Backblaze stores multiple copies of your data in different geographic locations, protecting against natural disasters, equipment failures, and other events that might affect a single data center.

Practical Backblaze Implementation

Install Backblaze on every computer your family uses for important work or storage. The per-computer pricing makes it affordable to protect multiple family computers with unlimited backup.

Configure Backblaze to back up external drives and network storage that contain important family files. The software can protect not just your computer's internal drive, but also connected storage devices.

Use Backblaze's mobile app to access your backed-up files from phones and tablets when you're away from home. This feature turns your backup into a personal cloud storage system.

Set up email notifications to confirm that backups are running successfully and alert you if any computers haven't been backed up recently.

Consider upgrading to Backblaze's extended version history if your family works with files that might be corrupted gradually. The longer retention periods provide additional protection against slowly developing problems.

Backblaze Limitations to Understand

Backblaze Personal Backup only protects computers, not phones or tablets. You'll need separate backup solutions for mobile devices, though most phones can back up automatically to iCloud or Google Drive.

The initial backup can take weeks or months if you have large amounts of data and a slow internet connection. Plan for this extended upload time when setting up Backblaze for the first time.

Restoring large amounts of data can be slow over internet connections. Backblaze offers optional physical drive shipping for large restores, but this service costs extra and takes several days.

The service is designed for backup, not file sharing or collaboration. While you can access your files remotely, Backblaze isn't a replacement for services like Google Drive or Dropbox designed for active file sharing.

> ★ **Pro Tip:** Backblaze offers an "inherit backup state" feature that lets you transfer backup history when replacing computers. This feature prevents you from starting over with a completely new backup when you get a new computer.

Backblaze represents the best balance of simplicity, affordability, and reliability for family backup needs. It's the backup solution I recommend most often because it gets used consistently instead of being set up and forgotten.

The "set it and forget it" nature of Backblaze makes it ideal for families who want comprehensive protection without ongoing maintenance or complex configuration. For most families, Backblaze should be the foundation of their backup strategy, supplemented by local backups and mobile device protection as needed.

What to Back Up (and What Not to): Making Smart Choices

Not all digital information deserves the same level of backup protection. Prioritizing your backup efforts helps you focus on protecting what's truly important while avoiding unnecessary costs and complexity.

High-Priority Backup Categories

Family photos and videos deserve the highest level of backup protection because they're irreplaceable and have enormous emotional value. These files should be backed up automatically to multiple locations with version history.

Financial documents, tax records, and legal papers need secure backup with long retention periods. These documents might be needed years later for audits, legal proceedings, or insurance claims.

Work files and business documents require backup strategies that meet your professional obligations and protect against career disruptions. Consider separate backup systems for work files if your employer requires specific security measures.

Personal documents like medical records, insurance policies, and identity documents should be backed up with strong encryption. These files often contain sensitive information that needs protection from unauthorized access.

Children's school projects, creative work, and personal files develop emotional value over time and should be included in family backup systems. Digital artwork, writing projects, and photos from childhood activities become treasured memories.

Low-Priority Backup Categories

Downloaded software and applications don't need backup because they can be re-downloaded from their original sources.

Focus backup resources on your personal data rather than replaceable software.

Cached files, temporary internet files, and system files consume storage space without providing value in backup systems. Configure backup software to exclude these categories automatically.

Streaming media and purchased digital content often don't need backup because they're available through your accounts with content providers. Netflix downloads and iTunes purchases can be re-downloaded when needed.

Large files that are easily recreated don't justify backup storage costs. Video game downloads, software installers, and other large files can often be obtained again more easily than they can be backed up.

Files that are already backed up elsewhere don't need duplicate protection. If your work files are backed up by your employer's systems, personal backup might be unnecessary redundancy.

Special Consideration Categories

Encrypted files and password-protected documents need special backup planning because they might not be recoverable without access to encryption keys or passwords. Document encryption methods and store recovery information securely.

Files with legal or regulatory requirements might need specific backup procedures, retention periods, and security measures. Consult with legal or compliance professionals for guidance on backing up sensitive business or personal documents.

Large media collections require cost-benefit analysis to determine appropriate backup levels. Professional photo libraries, video collections, and music archives might justify expensive backup solutions, while casual collections might not.

Files that change frequently need more sophisticated backup systems that can handle rapid updates without consuming excessive storage or bandwidth.

Shared files that multiple family members access need coordination to prevent conflicts and ensure that all changes are captured in backup systems.

> ■ **Danger Zone:** Never rely on a single backup method, no matter how reliable it seems. Multiple independent backup systems provide protection against the failure of any single backup approach.

Recovery Planning and Testing: When Backup Becomes Restoration

Having backups is only half of data protection; the other half is being able to restore data quickly and completely when disasters strike. Many families discover that their backup systems don't work only when they desperately need them.

Developing Recovery Procedures

Create step-by-step procedures for restoring data from each of your backup systems. Write these procedures down and store them separately from the devices they're meant to protect.

Test recovery procedures with small amounts of non-critical data before you need them for real emergencies. Practice restoring files, applications, and system settings to ensure you understand the process.

Document the information required for recovery operations: account passwords, recovery keys, contact information for support services, and locations of backup media.

Plan for different types of recovery scenarios: individual file recovery, complete device replacement, and disaster recovery when multiple devices are lost simultaneously.

Consider the time required for different types of recovery operations. Restoring large amounts of data from cloud storage might take days or weeks depending on your internet connection speed.

Recovery Testing Schedules

Schedule quarterly recovery tests to verify that your backup systems are working correctly and that you can restore data when needed. Regular testing identifies problems while there's still time to fix them.

Test different types of recovery operations: single file restoration, folder recovery, and complete system restoration. Each type of recovery exercises different parts of your backup system.

Involve different family members in recovery testing so that multiple people understand how to restore data during emergencies. Don't assume that only one person will always be available to handle recovery operations.

Document the results of recovery tests and use them to improve your backup and recovery procedures. Failed tests provide valuable information about weaknesses in your protection strategy.

Use recovery testing as an opportunity to verify that backup systems are including all the files and folders you think they're protecting.

Emergency Recovery Planning

Create emergency contact information for all your backup and cloud storage providers. Keep this information in multiple locations so you can access it even when your primary devices are unavailable.

Develop procedures for accessing backup systems from borrowed or replacement devices. You might need to restore data to unfamiliar computers during emergencies.

Plan for scenarios where primary recovery methods aren't available. If your internet connection is disrupted, how will you access cloud-based backups?

Consider the order of recovery operations when multiple devices need to be restored. Some devices might be more critical for daily operations and should be restored first.

Establish criteria for deciding when to restore data versus when to start over with new systems. Sometimes clean installation might be faster than recovering potentially corrupted systems.

Backing up your data requires ongoing commitment and periodic attention, but the protection it provides is invaluable. The time and money invested in proper backup systems pays for itself the first time you need to recover lost data.

Think of backup as insurance for your files and memories. You hope you never need it, but when disaster strikes, having comprehensive backup protection makes the difference between minor inconvenience and devastating loss.

But remember that backup is just one component of your family's overall digital security strategy. Protected data can still be stolen, and backed-up accounts can still be compromised. Backup protects against data loss, but it doesn't replace the need for strong security practices that prevent attacks in the first place.

Chapter 10: Safe Online Habits - Browsing, Shopping, and Socializing

---

The "I Love You" virus that crashed our company email at 4 AM

The pager went off at 4:17 AM with a message that made my blood run cold: "Email system down. CEO trying to reach you. URGENT."

I called the emergency number and heard panic in the CEO's voice. Our corporate email server was attempting to send hundreds of thousands of messages and grinding to a halt. The system was so overloaded that legitimate business communications couldn't get through.

Someone had opened an email attachment labeled "LOVE-LETTER-FOR-YOU.TXT.vbs" and unleashed the "I Love You" virus into our company network. The virus immediately sent itself to everyone in the infected person's address book. When those people opened it, the virus spread to their contacts. Within hours, our entire corporate communication system was paralyzed.

The virus didn't steal data or demand ransom. It just wanted to spread, and it succeeded because people trust messages that appear to come from friends and colleagues. The attack cost us tens of thousands of dollars in lost productivity and emergency IT support, all because one employee couldn't resist opening what looked like a love letter.

That incident taught me that human nature is often the weakest link in any security system. The best technical protections in the world can't save you from clicking on things you shouldn't click on.

Twenty-five years later, the threats have evolved but the fundamental problem remains the same: criminals design their attacks around predictable human behavior. They know you'll click links that seem to come from friends. They know you'll enter passwords on websites that look legitimate. They know you'll trust phone calls from people who sound official.

Your family's online safety depends more on developing good habits than on installing perfect software.

Modern Browsing Security: Navigating the Dangerous Web

The internet has become a minefield of malicious websites, fake download buttons, and deceptive advertisements designed to trick you into installing malware or revealing personal information. Modern browsing security requires both technical protection and educated decision-making.

Browser Security Configuration

Update your web browser regularly and enable automatic updates. Browsers receive security patches weekly to fix vulnerabilities that criminals actively exploit. An outdated browser is like leaving your front door unlocked.

Enable browser security features that block malicious websites, prevent dangerous downloads, and warn about suspicious activity. Chrome, Firefox, Safari, and Edge all include sophisticated protection systems that work automatically in the background.

Install ad blockers and tracking protection extensions to reduce exposure to malicious advertisements and privacy violations. Extensions like uBlock Origin block not just annoying ads, but also malicious ads that can infect your computer without any clicking required.

Configure your browser to ask before downloading files and to scan downloads for malware. Many browser infections happen through downloads that people didn't intend to start.

Disable or restrict browser plugins like Flash and Java that are common targets for criminal exploitation. Most modern websites work fine without these legacy plugins, and disabling them eliminates major attack vectors.

◆ **Personal Experience:** I discovered the power of ad blockers when helping a family whose computer was getting infected repeatedly despite having antivirus software. The infections were coming from malicious advertisements on legitimate news websites. Installing an ad blocker immediately stopped the infections and made their browsing experience faster and safer.

Recognizing Malicious Websites

Learn to identify websites that are designed to steal information or install malware. Look for obvious spelling errors, unprofessional design, urgent language demanding immediate action, and requests for unnecessary personal information.

Check website URLs carefully before entering sensitive information. Criminals create fake websites with URLs that look similar to legitimate sites: paypal-security.com instead of paypal.com, or amazon.com instead of amazon.com.

Be suspicious of websites that display excessive pop-up warnings about virus infections or system problems. Legitimate antivirus warnings come from your installed security software, not from websites you're visiting.

Avoid downloading software from unknown websites or clicking download buttons that appear in advertisements. Criminals often disguise malware as legitimate software or create fake download buttons that install malware instead of the software you wanted.

Look for secure connection indicators (https://) when entering personal information, but understand that criminals can also obtain security certificates for malicious websites. A secure connection means your information is encrypted during transmission, but it doesn't guarantee that the website itself is legitimate.

Safe Search and Information Gathering

Use reputable search engines that filter malicious results and warn about dangerous websites. Google, Bing, and other major search engines invest heavily in protecting users from search result manipulation.

Be cautious about clicking on sponsored search results or advertisements that appear at the top of search pages. Criminals often buy advertising space to promote malicious websites that appear legitimate.

Verify information from multiple sources before trusting important claims you find online. Misinformation and scam websites often rank highly in search results for trending topics or financial advice.

Use fact-checking websites and authoritative sources when researching important topics: medical information, financial advice, or news events. Wikipedia, government websites, and established news organizations provide more reliable information than random blogs or social media posts.

> ★ **Pro Tip:** Create a separate "online shopping" browser profile with strict security settings and no saved passwords. Use this profile only for e-commerce activities to isolate shopping-related risks from your daily browsing.

Be skeptical of websites that promise unrealistic benefits: miracle cures, get-rich-quick schemes, or exclusive insider information. These websites often collect personal information for identity theft or trick people into paying for worthless products.

Social Media Privacy for All Ages: Protecting Your Digital Identity

Social media platforms collect enormous amounts of personal information and share it in ways that most users don't understand. Each platform has different privacy policies, security features, and risks that require specific protection strategies.

Privacy Settings Configuration

Review and adjust privacy settings on all social media accounts annually. Platforms frequently change their privacy policies and add new data collection features that are often enabled by default.

Limit who can see your posts, contact you, and tag you in photos. Default privacy settings usually make your information more visible than necessary for personal use.

Disable location tracking and geotagging features that reveal where you live, work, and spend time. This location information can be used by criminals to plan physical crimes or by advertisers to create detailed profiles of your daily routines.

Review tagged photos and posts that mention you before they appear on your profile. Friends and family members might share information about you that you prefer to keep private.

Configure notification settings to alert you when someone tries to log into your accounts from new devices or unusual locations. These alerts help you detect unauthorized access quickly.

Information Sharing Guidelines

Think carefully before sharing personal information that could be used for identity theft: full birth dates, addresses, phone numbers, workplace information, or travel plans. Criminals piece together this information from multiple posts to build detailed profiles.

Avoid posting photos that reveal valuable possessions, home security details, or information about when your house is empty. Burglars use social media to identify targets and plan break-ins.

Be cautious about sharing children's information: school names, sports team affiliations, activity schedules, or photos that show school uniforms or team jerseys. This information can be used by predators to locate and approach children.

Consider the permanence of social media posts. Information you share today might be accessible for years and could affect your family's future opportunities or safety.

Use privacy-focused messaging apps for sensitive conversations instead of posting them on social media platforms where they might be stored indefinitely and shared with advertisers.

Managing Children's Social Media Use

Create age-appropriate social media accounts for children with strict privacy settings and parental oversight. Most platforms have minimum age requirements and offer enhanced protection for younger users.

Teach children about the permanence of online posts and the importance of thinking before sharing. Photos, comments, and posts that seem harmless today might cause problems years later.

Monitor children's friend lists and investigate requests from unknown adults or profiles that seem suspicious. Online predators often use fake profiles to contact children through social media.

Set up content filters and time limits for children's social media use. These controls help protect children from inappropriate content and prevent excessive social media use that interferes with sleep and schoolwork.

Have regular conversations about online experiences, both positive and negative. Children should feel comfortable reporting concerning interactions or content without fear of losing social media privileges.

A family discovered that their teenage daughter's Instagram posts were being used to create fake dating profiles on adult websites. Criminals had collected her photos and personal information from her public Instagram account and were using her identity to scam lonely men looking for relationships.

The fake profiles used the daughter's real photos but claimed she was 25 years old and looking for a serious relationship. The criminals were collecting money from men who thought they were talking to the daughter, creating a complex web of fraud and identity theft.

The family only discovered the problem when one of the men showed up at their house looking for his "girlfriend." The daughter had no idea her social media posts were being used for criminal purposes, and the fake profiles had been active for months before being discovered.

The incident demonstrated how public social media information can be weaponized in unexpected ways and why privacy settings matter even for seemingly innocent content.

Online Shopping and Financial Safety: Protecting Your Money

Online shopping has become essential for most families, but it also creates new opportunities for criminals to steal financial information and trick people into paying for goods that never arrive.

Secure Shopping Practices

Shop only on websites that use secure connections (https://) and have clear contact information, return policies, and customer service options. Legitimate retailers provide multiple ways to contact them and clear terms for returns and refunds.

Use credit cards instead of debit cards for online purchases. Credit cards provide stronger fraud protection and don't give criminals direct access to your bank account if the card information is stolen.

Shop through official retailer websites instead of clicking links in emails or advertisements. Criminals create fake shopping websites that look identical to legitimate retailers but steal your payment information.

Check your credit card statements regularly for unauthorized charges. Many fraudulent charges are small amounts that criminals hope you won't notice.

Save screenshots or confirmation emails for online purchases as proof of your transactions. This documentation helps resolve disputes if products don't arrive or charges appear incorrectly.

Payment Security

Use digital payment systems like Apple Pay, Google Pay, or PayPal when available. These services provide an extra layer of security by not sharing your actual credit card numbers with merchants.

Avoid storing payment information on shopping websites unless you use them frequently. Stored payment information can be stolen if the retailer's database is compromised.

Create strong, unique passwords for accounts on shopping websites and enable two-factor authentication when available. Shopping accounts often contain payment information and purchase history that criminals can exploit.

Monitor your credit reports for unauthorized accounts or changes that might indicate identity theft. Many credit monitoring services are available for free and can alert you to suspicious activity.

Set up account alerts for online banking and credit cards that notify you immediately when transactions occur. Quick notification helps you respond rapidly to unauthorized charges.

Avoiding Shopping Scams

Be suspicious of deals that seem too good to be true: luxury items at impossibly low prices, limited-time offers that pressure immediate action, or products that aren't available anywhere else.

Research unfamiliar retailers before making purchases. Check customer reviews, Better Business Bureau ratings, and search for complaints about the company.

> ▲ **Caution:** Never provide your Social Security number, driver's license number, or bank account information for online purchases. Legitimate retailers only need basic contact information and payment card details.

Avoid shopping websites that require unusual payment methods: wire transfers, cryptocurrency, gift cards, or money transfer services. Legitimate retailers accept standard credit and debit cards.

Be cautious about "free trial" offers that require credit card information. Many of these offers are subscription traps that charge your card repeatedly for products you don't want.

Watch for shipping and handling charges that seem excessive compared to the product price. Some scam websites offer low product prices but charge outrageous shipping fees.

Recognizing and Avoiding Modern Scams: The New Con Artists

Modern scammers use sophisticated psychological techniques and current events to create convincing fraud schemes. They understand human psychology better than most security experts and design their attacks to exploit natural emotional responses.

Email and Message Scams

Modern phishing emails look increasingly professional and often appear to come from legitimate companies or government agencies. They create urgency by claiming your account will be closed, your benefits will be suspended, or immediate action is required.

Check sender email addresses carefully. Criminals use addresses that look similar to legitimate organizations: support@arnazon.com instead of amazon.com, or notices@bankofamerica-security.net instead of the bank's real domain.

Be suspicious of emails requesting personal information, password verification, or immediate action. Legitimate companies rarely ask for sensitive information through email and don't create artificial deadlines for account actions.

Don't click links in suspicious emails. Instead, go directly to the organization's website by typing the URL in your browser or calling their customer service number.

Forward suspected phishing emails to the Anti-Phishing Working Group at reportphishing@apwg.org to help protect other people from the same scams.

Phone and Text Scams

Phone scammers have become more sophisticated and often know personal information about their targets that makes their calls seem legitimate. They might know your name, address, recent purchases, or financial information obtained from data breaches.

Be skeptical of unsolicited calls claiming to be from government agencies, tech support companies, or financial institutions. Legitimate organizations rarely call customers without prior contact or scheduled appointments.

Never provide personal information, passwords, or payment details to unsolicited callers. If someone claims to represent a company you do business with, hang up and call the company's official customer service number.

Don't trust caller ID information that shows familiar company names or government agencies. Criminals can fake caller ID to make their calls appear to come from trusted sources.

Be particularly cautious about calls creating artificial urgency: claims that your computer is infected, your benefits are suspended, or legal action is pending. These pressure tactics are designed to prevent you from thinking carefully about the request.

Romance and Social Engineering Scams

Online romance scams target lonely people through dating websites, social media, and gaming platforms. Scammers create fake profiles and spend months building emotional relationships before asking for money.

Be suspicious of online relationships that move quickly toward declarations of love or requests for personal information. Legitimate relationships develop gradually without pressure for immediate emotional commitment.

Never send money, gift cards, or personal information to someone you've only met online. Scammers often claim they need money for travel, medical emergencies, or temporary financial problems.

Be cautious about people who refuse to meet in person or always have excuses for why video calls aren't possible. Many romance scammers use stolen photos and can't provide real-time video proof of their identity.

Research photos and stories that seem too good to be true. Reverse image searches can reveal when profile photos are stolen from other sources.

Tech Support and Computer Scams

Criminals call random phone numbers claiming to be from Microsoft, Apple, or other technology companies and offer to fix computer problems that don't exist. They convince victims to install remote access software and then charge hundreds of dollars for unnecessary "repairs."

Never trust unsolicited calls about computer problems. Legitimate technology companies don't call customers to report issues with their computers.

Don't install software or allow remote access based on phone calls or pop-up messages claiming your computer is infected. Use only security software that you've chosen and installed yourself.

Be suspicious of pop-up messages claiming your computer has viruses or needs immediate attention. These fake warnings are designed to trick you into calling scammer phone numbers or downloading malware.

Real security warnings come from your installed antivirus software, not from websites or unsolicited phone calls.

> ■ **Danger Zone:** Never give remote access to your computer to anyone who contacted you first. Criminals can steal personal information, install malware, and access your financial accounts through remote access software.

Safe online habits protect your family more effectively than any security software because most attacks succeed by tricking people into making mistakes. Criminals count on families being busy, distracted, and trusting, but awareness and good habits can defeat even sophisticated scams.

The internet doesn't have to be a dangerous place if you understand how criminals operate and develop instincts for recognizing threats. Teaching your family to think critically about online communications and offers provides protection that adapts to new threats as they emerge.

But remember that safe online habits are just one component of your family's overall security strategy. Good browsing practices protect against many threats, but they need to be combined with strong passwords, regular backups, and secure device configuration to provide comprehensive protection.

PART V: Family and Multi-User Considerations

Chapter 11: Keeping Children Safe in the Digital World

The teenager whose cloud photos were shared with all her friends

---

Fifteen-year-old Madison Novak thought her photos were private when she stored them in her iCloud account. She'd taken some pictures in her bedroom that she considered personal but not inappropriate - trying on different outfits, making silly faces, and experimenting with makeup looks. They were the kind of photos teenagers take when they're figuring out their identity.

Madison had no idea that her iCloud account was set to share photos automatically with her family's shared photo library. When her younger brother logged into the family iPad to play games, all of Madison's "private" photos appeared in the shared album. The brother, thinking the photos were funny, showed them to his friends at school.

Within hours, Madison's personal photos were circulating among her classmates. Kids were taking screenshots and sharing them on social media. What started as innocent teenage self-expression became a humiliating privacy violation that followed Madison for months.

The technical problem was simple: a misconfigured iCloud setting that shared photos across family devices. But the emotional damage was devastating. Madison felt betrayed by technology she'd trusted, embarrassed by exposure she never intended, and angry at parents who hadn't explained how family sharing worked.

The incident taught the Novak family that children's digital privacy needs different protection than adult privacy. Kids don't understand the technical implications of sharing settings, and they don't anticipate how their private content might be exposed through family technology connections.

Your children's digital safety depends on creating protection systems that work even when kids make mistakes, share too much, or encounter threats they're not equipped to handle alone.

Age-Appropriate Device Settings: Growing Digital Boundaries

Children's device security needs evolve as they develop better judgment, technical skills, and understanding of digital consequences. The restrictions that protect a seven-year-old will frustrate a fourteen-year-old and may reduce security if they encourage workarounds.

Early Elementary (Ages 5-8): Foundation Building

Create completely supervised accounts with maximum restrictions and zero independent access to app stores, web browsing, or communication features. Young children should only use devices under direct adult supervision.

Disable all communication features: messaging, email, video calling, and social media. Children this age don't need to communicate digitally with anyone outside your immediate family.

Set extremely restrictive content filters that block all unmoderated content. Allow only pre-approved educational apps, games designed for young children, and streaming content from trusted sources like **PBS Kids** or **Disney+**.

Configure automatic logout after short periods of inactivity. Young children often walk away from devices without closing apps or logging out, creating opportunities for siblings or visitors to access their accounts.

Remove access to any features that involve spending money: app purchases, in-game transactions, or digital content stores. Young children don't understand the connection between virtual purchases and real money.

> ◆ **Personal Experience:** I helped a family whose six-year-old had downloaded 47 "free" games in one afternoon, each requiring parental approval. The child had learned to repeatedly ask "Can I download this game?" while showing the screen, not understanding that some games cost money. The parents approved requests without reading carefully and ended up with $200 in charges before realizing what was happening.

Late Elementary (Ages 9-12): Expanded Supervision

Introduce limited communication features with heavy monitoring and approval requirements. Children can start learning digital communication skills with training wheels still engaged.

Allow access to age-appropriate educational websites and pre-approved entertainment content. Begin teaching web browsing skills with strong content filters and regular discussion about what they encounter online.

Enable app downloads with parental approval for each installation. Children can start making technology choices with adult oversight and explanation of why certain apps are appropriate or inappropriate.

Set up basic time limits and usage schedules that prevent device use from interfering with sleep, homework, and family activities. Children need to learn healthy technology habits before gaining more independence.

Configure detailed activity monitoring that lets you see what websites they visit, what apps they use, and how much time they spend on different activities. Use this information for education and conversation, not just restriction.

Middle School (Ages 13-15): Guided Independence

Expand communication permissions to include messaging with known friends and family members. Children can start building digital social skills with boundaries that prevent contact with strangers.

Allow broader internet access with content filtering focused on blocking harmful material rather than restricting all unsupervised browsing. Teens need to learn to navigate the web safely with gradually reduced protection.

Introduce social media access with privacy settings locked to maximum protection and friend lists subject to parental review. Social media skills are essential for modern teens, but they need scaffolding to learn safe practices.

Implement spending controls and approval requirements for digital purchases. Teens can start learning money management skills in digital contexts with safeguards that prevent expensive mistakes.

Establish clear consequences for violating digital safety rules, but make consequences educational rather than purely punitive. The goal is building judgment, not just compliance.

High School (Ages 16-18): Preparation for Independence

Gradually reduce restrictions while maintaining open communication about digital choices and their consequences. Teens need practice making independent decisions before leaving home.

Allow more privacy in digital communications while retaining the ability to monitor for safety concerns. Respect growing independence while maintaining protective oversight.

Provide education about digital footprints, online reputation management, and the long-term consequences of digital choices. Teens need to understand how their online behavior might affect future opportunities.

Introduce more complex digital responsibilities: managing their own cloud storage, understanding privacy settings across multiple platforms, and protecting their own devices and accounts.

> ★ **Pro Tip:** Create a family technology agreement that evolves with your children's ages and demonstrates increasing trust as they show responsible digital behavior. Make it a conversation starter, not a legal document.

Begin teaching adult-level digital security skills: password management, recognizing sophisticated scams, and understanding the privacy implications of different technology choices.

Parental Controls Across Device Types: Technical Protection That Works

Effective parental controls require coordination across multiple devices and platforms because children often find ways around restrictions on individual devices by using other technology available in your home.

Router-Level Controls: The Foundation

Configure content filtering and time restrictions at your router level to create baseline protection that affects all devices on your network. Router-level controls work even when children use devices that don't have individual parental control apps.

Set up different user profiles for different family members with age-appropriate restrictions. Many modern routers can assign different rules to different devices based on MAC addresses or user accounts.

Block access to specific websites, categories of content, or entire domains that aren't appropriate for children. Router-level blocking works regardless of which browser or app children use to access the internet.

Configure time-based restrictions that automatically disable internet access for children's devices during homework time, family meals, and bedtime hours. These restrictions work even if children try to change settings on their individual devices.

Monitor network activity to identify new devices or unusual usage patterns that might indicate children are circumventing individual device restrictions.

iOS Parental Controls: Screen Time and Restrictions

Enable Screen Time with age-appropriate limits for different categories of apps and websites. Set daily time limits for entertainment apps while allowing unlimited access to educational content.

Configure App Limits that prevent installation of inappropriate apps and require approval for all app downloads. Review and approve app installation requests promptly to avoid frustrating children with legitimate needs.

Use Communication Limits to control who children can contact during different times of day. Allow contact with family members and approved friends while blocking communication with unknown people.

Set up Content & Privacy Restrictions that block inappropriate websites, prevent access to explicit content in iTunes and the App Store, and disable features like location sharing that create privacy risks.

Configure Family Sharing to manage children's purchases, share appropriate content across family devices, and maintain oversight of children's digital spending without creating unnecessary friction.

Android Parental Controls: Family Link Management

Set up Google Family Link accounts for children under 18 to manage app installations, screen time, device usage, and content filtering across Android devices.

Configure app approval requirements that send notification requests to parents when children want to install new apps. Review these requests promptly and use them as opportunities to discuss appropriate technology choices.

Establish bedtime and device locking schedules that automatically lock children's devices during sleep hours and family time. These controls work even if children try to change local device settings.

Monitor activity reports that show which apps children use most, what websites they visit, and how much time they spend on different activities. Use this information for conversation and guidance rather than punishment.

Set location tracking for safety purposes while respecting children's growing need for independence. Location tracking can help ensure children are where they're supposed to be without being invasive about their activities.

Gaming Console Controls: Entertainment Protection

Configure parental controls on gaming consoles to prevent access to inappropriate games, limit online communication with strangers, and control spending on digital content.

Set up separate child accounts with appropriate content ratings and spending limits. Gaming platforms often have solid parental control features that are more effective than trying to monitor adult accounts used by children.

Monitor friend lists and communication features to ensure children aren't contacted by inappropriate people through gaming platforms. Review friend requests and investigate any adult contacts or suspicious usernames.

Control access to user-generated content in games that allow players to create and share custom content. User-generated content often bypasses content rating systems and can expose children to inappropriate material.

> ▲ **Caution:** Parental controls are tools for protection and education, not substitutes for communication and trust. Children who feel overly restricted often find ways to circumvent controls or engage in risky behavior when restrictions are lifted.

Establish clear rules about online gaming behavior and communication with other players. Gaming platforms can expose children to cyberbullying, inappropriate language, and predatory behavior.

Teaching Digital Citizenship: Building Character Online

Digital citizenship education teaches children to behave ethically, safely, and responsibly in online environments. The goal is developing internal guidance systems that work even when external controls aren't present.

Understanding Digital Footprints

Teach children that everything they post online becomes part of a permanent record that might be accessible years later. Help them understand that employers, colleges, and future relationships might judge them based on their digital history.

Show children how to search for themselves online and understand what information about them is publicly available. This exercise helps them understand the concept of digital reputation and the importance of managing their online presence.

Explain how digital content can be copied, screenshot, and shared without their permission. Children need to understand that "private" messages and "temporary" content can become permanent and public unexpectedly.

Help children understand the difference between their intended audience for digital content and their actual audience. A post meant for close friends might be seen by extended family, school administrators, or future employers.

Practice thinking through the long-term consequences of different types of digital content before posting. Develop family habits of pausing to consider whether content is appropriate for the widest possible audience.

Respecting Others Online

Teach children that online communication should follow the same rules of kindness and respect that apply to face-to-face interactions. The anonymity of digital communication doesn't excuse cruel or inappropriate behavior.

Help children understand that people online are real people with real feelings, even when they're represented by usernames, avatars, or profiles that seem artificial or distant.

Establish family rules about cyberbullying, harassment, and inappropriate content sharing. Make it clear that participating in or amplifying cruel behavior online is unacceptable regardless of whether your child initiated it.

Teach children to think carefully before sharing other people's content, photos, or personal information. Respect for others' privacy and dignity should guide digital sharing decisions.

Practice empathy by helping children consider how their online actions might affect other people's feelings, reputation, or safety.

Critical Thinking About Online Information

Teach children to question information they encounter online and to verify important claims through multiple reliable sources. Digital literacy includes understanding the difference between facts, opinions, and misinformation.

Help children understand how advertising, sponsored content, and algorithmic recommendations influence what they see online. They need to recognize when content is designed to sell them something or manipulate their emotions.

Explain how echo chambers and filter bubbles can create false impressions about what most people believe or how the world really works. Encourage children to seek diverse perspectives and challenge their own assumptions.

Practice identifying reliable sources of information and distinguishing between authoritative content and random opinions or deliberate misinformation.

Teach children to be skeptical of sensational claims, conspiracy theories, and content that seems designed to make them angry or afraid.

A middle school teacher created a fake social media controversy about whether the school should ban chocolate milk from the cafeteria. Students passionate about chocolate milk began sharing increasingly exaggerated claims about the health benefits and dangers of chocolate milk.

After a week of heated online debate, the teacher revealed that she'd created the entire controversy using fake accounts and manipulated information. The students were shocked to realize how easily they'd been manipulated and how quickly reasonable people could become polarized over a trivial issue.

The exercise taught the students to recognize manipulation tactics, question the sources of controversial information, and think critically about their own emotional responses to online content. It was more effective than any theoretical lesson about media literacy because the students experienced firsthand how misinformation spreads and influences behavior.

Balancing Monitoring with Privacy: Building Trust While Staying Safe

The challenge of children's digital safety is providing adequate protection without destroying the trust and independence that children need to develop healthy relationships with technology.

Age-Appropriate Privacy Expectations

Young children (elementary age) shouldn't expect digital privacy from parents. Complete transparency about digital activities is appropriate and necessary for safety at this age.

Middle school children can have limited privacy for peer communication while maintaining parental oversight of safety-related activities. Privacy becomes a privilege earned through responsible behavior.

High school students deserve increasing privacy as they demonstrate good judgment and responsible digital behavior. Privacy restrictions should focus on safety rather than control as teens approach adulthood.

Create clear family policies about when and why parents will access children's digital communications. Emergency situations, safety concerns, and violations of family rules justify increased monitoring.

Explain the reasoning behind monitoring decisions so children understand the difference between invasive snooping and protective oversight.

Building Trust Through Communication

Have regular conversations about digital experiences without making every discussion feel like an interrogation. Children should feel comfortable sharing both positive and concerning online experiences.

Respond to children's digital mistakes with education and problem-solving rather than punishment and restriction. The goal is helping children develop better judgment, not perfect compliance with rules.

Create opportunities for children to demonstrate responsible digital behavior and earn increased privileges and independence. Trust should grow in response to demonstrated responsibility.

Be transparent about your own digital challenges and mistakes. Children learn more from seeing how adults handle digital dilemmas than from lectures about perfect behavior.

Acknowledge when your monitoring or restrictions were unnecessary and adjust your approach based on children's growing maturity and demonstrated judgment.

Responding to Digital Safety Incidents

Develop family procedures for handling online safety problems: cyberbullying, inappropriate contact, exposure to harmful content, or violations of family technology rules.

Create non-punitive reporting systems that encourage children to come to you when they encounter problems online. Children should never fear losing technology privileges for reporting safety concerns.

Focus on problem-solving and learning when digital incidents occur rather than assigning blame or implementing blanket restrictions that might prevent children from developing independent judgment.

Document serious incidents and involve schools, law enforcement, or other authorities when appropriate. Some online threats require professional intervention beyond family responses.

Use these incidents as teaching opportunities for the entire family. Other children can learn from their siblings' experiences without having to make the same mistakes.

> ■ **Danger Zone:** Never use monitoring tools to spy on children's normal social development or to control age-appropriate exploration of independence. Overly invasive monitoring can damage parent-child relationships and prevent children from developing healthy boundaries.

Children's digital safety requires a combination of technical protection, ongoing education, and evolving trust that grows with children's demonstrated responsibility. The goal isn't perfect control over children's digital experiences, but rather preparation for them to make safe, ethical, and responsible choices as independent adults.

The effort you invest in teaching digital citizenship and building appropriate monitoring systems pays dividends when children encounter situations you haven't anticipated and need to rely on their own judgment to stay safe.

But remember that children's online safety is embedded in your family's overall approach to technology and communication. Children learn more from observing how their parents handle digital challenges than from any formal rules or restrictions you implement.

Chapter 12: Supporting Family Members Who Struggle with Technology

---

The grandmother whose birth date bank password was obvious to thieves

---

Seventy-three-year-old Eleanor Matsumoto used her birth date as the password for everything: her email, her bank account, her social media, and her online shopping accounts. The password was 02121951 - her birthday in plain numbers with no variations or additions.

Eleanor's granddaughter had repeatedly tried to explain why birth date passwords were dangerous, but Eleanor found other password requirements confusing and impossible to remember. She'd written down more complex passwords but forgot where she'd put the paper. She'd tried password managers but couldn't figure out how to use them. The birth date password was the only system that worked for her daily needs.

Criminals didn't need sophisticated hacking tools to access Eleanor's accounts. Her birth date was listed on her Facebook profile, appeared in public records, and was known to dozens of acquaintances. Once criminals had this password, they gained access to her entire digital life in minutes.

The attack drained Eleanor's checking account, opened three credit cards in her name, and used her email to scam her friends and family. The financial damage totaled $18,000, but the emotional impact was worse. Eleanor felt stupid, violated, and afraid to use any technology without constant supervision.

Eleanor's story isn't unusual. Millions of seniors and less technical family members use security practices that make them easy targets for criminals. They're not careless or foolish;

they're using technology that wasn't designed for their needs and abilities.

Your family's digital security is only as strong as its least technical member. The most sophisticated security setup in the world won't protect your family if one member's weak password gives criminals access to shared accounts and family information.

Understanding Different Technical Comfort Levels

Family members with different ages, backgrounds, and experience levels need different approaches to digital security. A solution that works perfectly for a tech-savvy teenager might be completely unusable for a grandparent who struggles with basic computer operation.

Identifying Technical Limitations

Observe how different family members interact with technology to understand their specific challenges and limitations. Some people struggle with fine motor control that makes typing difficult. Others have vision problems that make small text hard to read. Memory issues can make complex procedures impossible to follow consistently.

Physical limitations affect security capabilities. Arthritis might make complex passwords impossible to type. Vision problems might make it difficult to distinguish between legitimate and fraudulent websites. Hearing difficulties might make phone-based two-factor authentication challenging.

Cognitive processing differences influence how people learn and remember security procedures. Some family members need step-by-step written instructions, while others learn better through hands-on demonstration. Some prefer simple rules they can apply consistently, while others want to understand the reasoning behind security recommendations.

> ◆ **Personal Experience:** I helped a family whose 80-year-old grandfather was getting scammed repeatedly because he trusted anyone who called claiming to be from "computer support." He'd grown up in an era when businesses didn't make unsolicited sales calls, so he assumed anyone who called with technical help was legitimate. Teaching him to be suspicious of helpful strangers required retraining a lifetime of social expectations.

Adapting Security Measures to Abilities

Design security systems that work within each person's actual capabilities rather than expecting everyone to adapt to optimal security practices. A password that's easy for a grandparent to remember and type might be more secure than a complex password they write down or share with others.

Simplify security procedures to their essential components. Perfect security that nobody can use provides no protection. Practical security that family members can implement consistently protects against real threats.

Setting Up Simplified Security for Seniors

Senior family members need security systems that prioritize usability over theoretical perfection. The goal is protection that gets used consistently rather than optimal security that gets abandoned when it becomes inconvenient.

Password Management for Seniors

Choose password strategies that work with seniors' memory capabilities and physical limitations. A password manager might be ideal, but a written password book might be more practical for someone who struggles with digital interfaces.

Create password systems that are both secure and memorable for each individual. "Eleanor's favorite vacation spot from 1975!" might be more secure than a random string of characters if Eleanor can remember it consistently and criminals can't guess it easily.

Set up password recovery systems that don't require technical knowledge or perfect memory. Security questions with answers that seniors can remember reliably work better than complex recovery procedures.

Use biometric authentication when it works reliably for seniors' physical characteristics. Fingerprint readers work well for some seniors but might not work reliably for people with worn fingerprints or skin conditions.

Write down passwords in secure locations when necessary. A password book kept in a home safe might be more secure than weak passwords that seniors can remember without help.

Simplified Two-Factor Authentication

Choose two-factor authentication methods that work reliably with seniors' devices and capabilities. Text message codes might be easier for seniors to use than authenticator apps, even though they're technically less secure.

Set up backup authentication methods that don't require perfect execution of primary methods. Backup codes printed in large fonts and stored securely provide alternatives when primary 2FA methods fail.

Configure 2FA systems to minimize false alarms and confusing prompts. Seniors might approve malicious authentication requests if they're confused about when and why they receive 2FA prompts.

Use trusted device features that reduce the frequency of 2FA prompts without completely eliminating protection. Marking home computers as trusted devices reduces authentication friction for daily activities.

Provide clear written instructions for 2FA procedures with large fonts and simple language. Include screenshots and step-by-step procedures that assume no prior technical knowledge.

Device Configuration for Senior Safety

Configure devices with security settings that work automatically rather than requiring ongoing management. Automatic updates, automatic backups, and automatic security scanning protect seniors without requiring technical maintenance.

Simplify device interfaces to reduce confusion and minimize opportunities for security mistakes. Remove unnecessary apps, organize remaining apps logically, and create shortcuts for frequently used security features.

Set up automatic logout features that protect accounts when seniors forget to log out of sensitive websites. Shorter timeout periods provide security without requiring perfect memory of logout procedures.

Configure spam filtering and call blocking to reduce exposure to scams and fraudulent communications. Technical solutions that block threats automatically work better than expecting seniors to identify and avoid all scams.

Use parental control features to protect seniors from malicious websites and dangerous downloads. Age-appropriate content filtering can protect seniors just as effectively as it protects children.

Here's an elegant senior security solution I implemented. An 85-year-old woman was getting overwhelmed by password requirements but refused to stop using her computer for email and online banking. Her family was considering taking away her computer access for her own protection.

Instead, I set up a dedicated computer for her banking and important accounts with extreme security measures: automatic logout after five minutes, access only to pre-approved websites, and monitoring software that detected unusual activity. For her casual internet use, I gave her a separate tablet with minimal security requirements.

The two-device approach let her maintain independence for low-risk activities while providing maximum protection for high-risk financial activities. She could check Facebook and play games on the tablet without worrying about security, but her banking was protected by systems she didn't need to understand or manage.

The solution worked because it matched security levels to risk levels and didn't require her to make complex security decisions during routine activities.

When to Call for Professional Help

Some digital security challenges require expertise beyond what most families can provide themselves. Recognizing when to seek professional help prevents small problems from becoming major disasters.

Signs You Need Professional Assistance

Call for help when family members experience repeated security incidents despite your best efforts to provide protection. Multiple password compromises, frequent malware infections, or ongoing scam victimization indicate that family-level solutions aren't sufficient.

Seek professional assistance when technical problems exceed your family's troubleshooting capabilities. Computers that behave strangely, network problems that affect multiple devices, or security software that doesn't work properly might require expert diagnosis.

Consider professional help when family members feel overwhelmed by security requirements and start avoiding technology altogether. Professional trainers can often explain security concepts in ways that make them more accessible and less intimidating.

Get expert assistance when legal or financial consequences of security incidents exceed your family's ability to resolve them independently. Identity theft recovery, fraud investigation, and interaction with law enforcement often require professional guidance.

Call for help when security incidents affect business or professional activities. Workplace security compromises might require specialized expertise and could have legal implications that need professional handling.

Types of Professional Security Services

Computer repair services can diagnose and fix malware infections, configure security software, and restore systems after security incidents. Choose services with specific cybersecurity expertise rather than general computer repair.

Cybersecurity consultants can assess your family's overall security posture, recommend improvements, and provide training tailored to your family's specific needs and technical capabilities.

Identity theft resolution services help families recover from compromised personal information, credit fraud, and financial account takeovers. These services handle the complex paperwork and communications required for recovery.

Elder fraud specialists understand the specific tactics used to target seniors and can provide both prevention education and incident response for families dealing with senior-targeted scams.

Digital forensics experts can investigate security incidents to determine what information was compromised and help prevent similar incidents in the future.

Choosing Reliable Security Help

Research service providers' credentials, certifications, and customer reviews before trusting them with your family's sensitive information. Cybersecurity is an unregulated industry with many unqualified providers.

Get detailed written estimates for security services before agreeing to work. Legitimate providers should be able to explain what they'll do, how long it will take, and what it will cost.

Avoid door-to-door or unsolicited offers for security services. Criminals often pose as security experts to gain access to homes and computers for malicious purposes.

Check references and verify business licenses for any service providers who will have access to your home or personal information. Security service providers should be more trustworthy than average service providers, not less.

Maintain oversight of professional security work and don't give unlimited access to your devices or accounts. Even legitimate service providers should work under supervision and with limited permissions.

> ★ **Pro Tip:** Before calling for professional help, document the specific problems you're experiencing and what you've tried to fix them. This information helps professionals diagnose issues more quickly and avoid repeating unsuccessful solutions.

Keeping Everyone Updated and Secure

Family digital security requires ongoing maintenance and education that accounts for different family members' changing needs, capabilities, and threat exposure.

Creating Sustainable Update Schedules

Establish regular family technology reviews that assess security settings, update procedures, and identify emerging risks. Monthly or quarterly reviews work better than waiting for problems to develop.

Assign age and skill-appropriate security maintenance tasks to different family members. Tech-savvy teenagers can help with software updates, while adults handle password management and account monitoring.

Create simple checklists for security maintenance tasks that less technical family members can follow independently. Written procedures with screenshots help ensure that security tasks get completed correctly.

Set up automatic systems for security maintenance whenever possible. Automatic updates, automatic backups, and automatic security scans reduce the maintenance burden for less technical family members.

Build security updates into existing family routines. Monthly password reviews during family meetings or quarterly device cleanups during seasonal cleaning make security maintenance more likely to happen consistently.

Education and Communication

Provide ongoing security education that adapts to family members' growing technical skills and emerging threats. Security education needs to evolve as both technology and family capabilities change.

Create safe spaces for family members to ask questions about security without feeling judged or criticized for their technical limitations. Fear of appearing stupid prevents many people from seeking help with security problems.

Share security success stories and lessons learned from security incidents. Family members learn more from concrete examples than from abstract security principles.

Encourage family members to report security concerns and suspicious activities without fear of blame or loss of technology privileges. Early reporting often prevents minor problems from becoming major disasters.

Keep security education current with emerging threats and changing technology. Security advice that worked five years ago might not address current risks or take advantage of new protection options.

Adapting to Changing Needs

Recognize that family members' security needs and capabilities change as they age, gain experience, or face new health challenges. Security systems need to evolve with changing family circumstances.

Consider the long-term sustainability of security approaches as family members age or develop health problems. Security systems that work today might not work when family members face physical or cognitive challenges.

> ▲ **Caution:** Never make family members feel helpless or incompetent about technology. Security education should build confidence and capability, not create dependence on others for basic digital activities.

Prepare for emergency situations where primary security contacts might not be available. Backup plans and emergency contacts help ensure that security incidents can be handled even when key family members are unavailable.

Document security procedures and access information so that multiple family members can handle security maintenance and incident response. Single points of failure in security management create vulnerabilities that criminals can exploit.

Building Inclusive Family Security

Effective family digital security includes everyone regardless of their technical skill level. The goal is creating protection systems that work for your family's actual capabilities rather than theoretical ideal users.

Accommodating Different Learning Styles

Provide security education in multiple formats to accommodate different learning preferences. Some people learn better from written instructions, others from hands-on demonstration, and still others from video tutorials.

Recognize and celebrate security successes when family members demonstrate good security practices or successfully handle security challenges. Positive reinforcement builds long-term security habits more effectively than criticism of mistakes.

Creating Security Support Networks

Establish buddy systems where more technical family members support less technical family members with security tasks. Pairing people creates redundancy and reduces the burden on any single family member.

> ■ **Danger Zone:** Never completely take over technology management for family members who are capable of learning basic security skills. Dependence on others for basic digital security creates single points of failure and reduces personal autonomy.

Supporting family members with different technical skill levels requires patience, creativity, and a willingness to adapt security practices to real human capabilities. Perfect security that nobody can use provides no protection. Practical security that everyone can implement successfully protects against real threats.

PART VI: Staying Secure in a Changing World

Chapter 13: Recognizing an Attack in Progress

The computer secretly working for criminals for months

The Patel family's computer had been acting sluggish for months, but they attributed it to the machine getting older and accumulating digital clutter. The fans ran constantly, the hard drive made grinding noises, and web pages loaded slowly. They planned to replace the computer eventually but saw no reason to rush.

What they didn't know was that their computer had been recruited into a cryptocurrency mining botnet six months earlier. Criminals were using their processor and electricity to generate digital currency while the family slept. The computer was working harder for criminals than it was for the Patel family.

The infection had started with a fake software update that appeared while their teenage son was downloading music. The malware installed silently and began communicating with criminal servers immediately. It downloaded additional software, joined a network of thousands of infected computers, and started mining cryptocurrency during idle periods.

The criminals were careful not to interfere with the family's normal computer use. The mining software reduced its activity when family members were actively using the computer, making the infection less obvious. The Patels noticed their computer was slower, but the degradation was gradual enough that they adapted to it without realizing something was wrong.

The infection was discovered only when their internet service provider sent a notice about unusual data usage. The computer had uploaded terabytes of data to suspicious servers, triggering automated monitoring systems. By then, the infection had been active for eight months and had cost the family hundreds of dollars in excess electricity and internet charges.

Most families don't realize when their devices are compromised because modern attacks are designed to be invisible. Criminals make more money from long-term access to your devices than from obvious attacks that get detected and cleaned up quickly.

Common Attack Scenarios for Home Users

Family-targeted attacks follow predictable patterns because criminals understand how most households use technology. Recognizing these patterns helps you identify problems before they cause serious damage.

The Slow Takeover: Gradual System Compromise

Many attacks succeed by gradually taking control of devices over weeks or months. The infection starts with a small foothold and slowly expands its access and capabilities without triggering obvious symptoms.

Initial compromise often happens through email attachments, fake software updates, or infected downloads that family members don't recognize as malicious. The initial infection might be small and undetectable by most security software.

The infection establishes persistence by hiding in system files, creating scheduled tasks, and modifying startup procedures. These changes ensure that the malware survives restarts and security scans.

Criminals expand their access by stealing passwords, escalating privileges, and installing additional tools. A simple trojan might evolve into a comprehensive surveillance and theft operation over several months.

The attack remains hidden by mimicking legitimate system processes, limiting resource usage during active hours, and avoiding activities that would trigger security alerts.

Family members might notice gradual performance degradation, occasional strange behavior, or minor anomalies, but they often attribute these symptoms to normal computer aging rather than security compromises.

The Emergency Scam: Creating Artificial Urgency

Criminals create fake emergencies that pressure families into making security mistakes under time pressure. These attacks exploit the natural human tendency to act quickly when faced with apparent crises.

Fake security warnings claim your computer is infected and provide phone numbers for "immediate technical support." The warnings look professional and often include legitimate-seeming company logos and official language.

Phishing emails claim your bank account has been compromised and require immediate password verification to prevent further damage. The emails create urgency by threatening account closure or legal action if you don't respond quickly.

Phone calls from "law enforcement" claim family members are in legal trouble and need immediate payment for bail, fines, or legal fees. The callers use official-sounding language and pressure tactics to prevent victims from verifying the claims.

Text messages claiming to be from family members report emergencies and request immediate financial help. The messages often include enough personal information to seem legitimate while creating pressure to act before verification.

Fake technical support calls claim to have detected security problems and offer immediate help for a fee. The callers often know enough about your computer setup to sound legitimate while pressuring you to allow remote access.

The Insider Attack: Trusted Access Gone Wrong

Some of the most damaging attacks come from people who have legitimate access to your home or devices: household workers, repair technicians, visitors, or even family members who abuse their trusted status.

Household workers with access to your home might install surveillance software on computers, copy files from devices, or use your internet connection for illegal activities while you're away.

Repair technicians might install backdoors in devices they're supposed to fix, copy personal files during legitimate repairs, or use service visits as opportunities to gather intelligence for future attacks.

Visitors might connect infected devices to your network, install malware through USB drives, or use temporary access to your devices to steal passwords and personal information.

Family members might accidentally compromise security by sharing passwords with friends, downloading infected software, or falling for social engineering attacks that affect the entire household.

Service providers might leave backdoors in systems they install, use administrative access for unauthorized purposes, or fail to remove temporary access when service relationships end.

The Social Engineering Assault: Psychological Manipulation

Modern criminals understand psychology better than most security professionals. They design attacks around predictable human responses to authority, fear, greed, and social pressure.

Authority-based attacks use fake credentials, official-looking communications, and bureaucratic language to make victims comply with unreasonable requests. People naturally defer to apparent authority figures even when the requests don't make sense.

Fear-based attacks threaten consequences like account closure, legal action, or security breaches to pressure victims into acting quickly without thinking carefully about the requests.

Greed-based attacks offer unrealistic benefits like free money, exclusive deals, or investment opportunities to entice victims into providing personal information or making payments.

Social pressure attacks use fake relationships, false emergencies involving family members, or claims about social connections to manipulate victims into helping supposed friends or relatives.

Curiosity-based attacks use interesting headlines, celebrity gossip, or shocking news stories to entice victims into clicking malicious links or downloading infected files.

> ★ **Pro Tip:** When someone creates urgency around a security or financial decision, that urgency itself is often a warning sign of a scam. Legitimate emergencies rarely require immediate action without verification.

What to Do When Something Goes Wrong

The first few minutes after discovering a security incident often determine how much damage occurs and how quickly you can recover. Having a planned response helps you act effectively when you're stressed and confused.

Immediate Response: Stop the Bleeding

Disconnect affected devices from the internet immediately to prevent further data theft and stop criminals from accessing your accounts remotely. Unplug ethernet cables or turn off WiFi connections on compromised devices.

Change passwords for all accounts that might have been accessed from compromised devices. Start with banking, email, and social media accounts that could be used to access other accounts or steal personal information.

Contact your bank and credit card companies to report potential fraud and request account monitoring. Many financial institutions can place temporary holds on accounts while you assess the extent of the compromise.

Document what you know about the incident: when you first noticed problems, what symptoms you observed, and what actions you've taken in response. This information helps technical support and law enforcement understand the scope of the attack.

Notify other family members about the incident so they can check their own accounts and devices for signs of compromise. Attacks often spread through family networks and shared accounts.

Assessment: Understanding the Damage

Determine which devices were affected by checking for unusual activity, changed settings, or new software installations on all family computers, phones, and tablets.

Review account activity logs for all online services to identify unauthorized access, changed settings, or suspicious transactions. Most services provide detailed logs of login times, locations, and activities.

Check for unauthorized purchases, new accounts opened in family members' names, or other financial fraud that might have resulted from stolen personal information.

Monitor credit reports for all family members to identify identity theft activities that might not be immediately obvious through account monitoring.

Examine home network activity to determine if other devices might be compromised or if criminals still have access to your internet connection.

A family discovered their computer was infected when their bank called about suspicious wire transfers. Instead of panicking, they followed a systematic response plan they'd developed after a previous minor incident.

First, they disconnected all devices from the internet and took photos of any suspicious activity on their screens. Then, they called their bank, credit card companies, and credit monitoring services to report potential fraud. They documented everything they found and took their infected computer to a forensics expert.

The systematic response limited their financial losses to $200 and helped law enforcement track down the criminals. Most importantly, they learned exactly how the attack had succeeded and implemented better security measures to prevent similar incidents.

Their methodical approach turned a potential disaster into a learning experience that made their family more secure in the long run.

Containment: Preventing Further Damage

Isolate infected devices and accounts to prevent the attack from spreading to other family members or devices. Change passwords from clean devices rather than potentially compromised ones.

Scan all family devices for malware using up-to-date security software from clean boot media when possible. Infections often spread through shared networks and storage devices.

Review and revoke access permissions for all online accounts, removing connections to third-party apps and services that might have been compromised during the attack.

Monitor bank and credit card statements daily for several weeks after an incident to catch delayed fraud attempts that might not appear immediately.

Consider professional forensic analysis for serious incidents that involve financial fraud, identity theft, or extensive system compromise. Professional analysis might reveal the full scope of the attack and provide evidence for law enforcement.

Recovery: Getting Back to Normal

Rebuild compromised systems from clean backups when possible rather than trying to clean infected systems that might retain hidden malware or backdoors.

Change all passwords using a clean device and implement stronger authentication for all accounts that were potentially compromised during the incident.

Update security software, operating systems, and applications on all devices to ensure that vulnerabilities used in the attack are patched.

Review and strengthen security practices that might have contributed to the successful attack. Use the incident as motivation to implement better security measures across your family's digital life.

Monitor all accounts and systems more closely for several months after an incident to ensure that the attack has been completely eliminated and hasn't resurged.

> ▲ **Caution:** Don't assume that removing visible malware has completely cleaned an infected system. Professional criminals often install multiple layers of malware and backdoors that require complete system rebuilding to eliminate.

Reporting Incidents and Getting Help

Security incidents affecting families often require professional assistance and law enforcement involvement, especially when financial fraud or identity theft occurs.

When to Contact Law Enforcement

Report incidents involving financial fraud, identity theft, or crimes against children to local law enforcement and appropriate federal agencies. These crimes require professional investigation and prosecution.

Contact the FBI's Internet Crime Complaint Center (IC3.gov) for incidents involving significant financial losses, organized crime, or attacks that cross state boundaries. Federal agencies have resources and jurisdiction that local police might lack.

Report business email compromise, ransomware attacks, and incidents affecting work devices to both law enforcement and your employer's security team. Workplace incidents might have legal and regulatory implications beyond personal consequences.

Document criminal threats, harassment, or extortion attempts with screenshots and detailed records. This evidence supports law enforcement investigation and prosecution efforts.

File reports even for unsuccessful attacks or attempts that didn't result in financial losses. Pattern recognition across multiple reports helps law enforcement identify and disrupt criminal operations.

Professional Assistance Resources

Contact cybersecurity professionals for incident response when attacks exceed your family's technical capabilities or when you need forensic analysis of compromised systems.

Use identity theft resolution services that specialize in helping families recover from compromised personal information and financial fraud. These services handle complex paperwork and coordination with multiple agencies.

Consult with attorneys when security incidents involve potential legal liability, workplace implications, or significant financial losses that might require litigation.

Work with credit monitoring services and financial institutions that offer specialized assistance for fraud victims and identity theft recovery.

Consider professional counseling for family members who experience emotional trauma from privacy violations, financial fraud, or other serious security incidents.

Building Support Networks

Establish relationships with local cybersecurity professionals before you need emergency assistance. Having trusted contacts makes crisis response more effective and reduces the risk of falling victim to fraudulent "help" services.

Connect with other families who have experienced similar security incidents through community groups, online forums, or victim support organizations. Shared experiences provide emotional support and practical advice.

> ■ **Danger Zone:** Be extremely cautious about unsolicited offers of help after security incidents. Criminals often target recent attack victims with follow-up scams claiming to provide recovery services or additional protection.

Maintain relationships with law enforcement cybercrime specialists in your area. Many police departments have officers who specialize in technology crimes and can provide guidance even for incidents that don't require formal investigation.

Document your support network contact information and keep it accessible from multiple locations. Security incidents often limit access to your normal communication methods and digital resources.

Learning from Security Failures

Security incidents provide valuable learning opportunities that can strengthen your family's future protection if you analyze them systematically and implement appropriate improvements.

Conducting Post-Incident Analysis

Determine how the attack succeeded by tracing the timeline from initial compromise to discovery. Understanding attack vectors helps prevent similar incidents in the future.

Identify security weaknesses that contributed to the successful attack: outdated software, weak passwords, missing security controls, or family behavior that created vulnerabilities.

Evaluate the effectiveness of your incident response procedures and identify areas for improvement. What worked well? What could have been done better or faster?

Assess the adequacy of your backup and recovery systems. Did backups work as expected? Were recovery procedures sufficient to restore normal operations quickly?

Review the support resources you used during the incident and evaluate their effectiveness. Which services were helpful? What additional resources might be needed for future incidents?

Implementing Lessons Learned

Update security policies and procedures based on what you learned from the incident. New threats often require new protection strategies that weren't necessary before.

Strengthen security controls that failed during the attack. Install additional protection layers, improve monitoring capabilities, or implement new authentication requirements.

Provide additional security education to family members based on the specific mistakes or vulnerabilities that contributed to the successful attack.

Test your improved security measures to ensure they work effectively and don't create new problems or usability issues that might lead to circumvention.

Document your lessons learned and share them with other families who might benefit from your experience. Security knowledge sharing helps protect entire communities.

Building Resilience

Accept that future security incidents are inevitable and focus on building resilience rather than trying to achieve perfect prevention. Strong recovery capabilities often matter more than perfect protection.

Develop incident response procedures that account for the specific types of attacks that have succeeded against your family in the past. Tailor your response plans to realistic threats.

Create redundant systems for critical functions so that security incidents don't completely disrupt your family's daily activities. Alternative communication methods, backup financial access, and emergency procedures maintain family functioning during crisis response.

Practice incident response procedures regularly so that family members can execute them effectively during actual emergencies when stress and confusion make clear thinking difficult.

Maintain perspective about security risks and don't let fear of future incidents prevent your family from benefiting from technology. The goal is reasonable protection, not paranoid isolation.

Effective response to security threats requires preparation, practice, and the willingness to learn from both successes and failures. The families that handle incidents most effectively are those who plan for problems before they occur and treat each one as a learning opportunity.

Your family's security will be tested eventually. The question isn't whether you'll face cyber threats, but whether you'll be prepared to recognize them quickly and respond effectively when they occur.

Remember that perfect security is impossible, but effective incident response can minimize damage and accelerate recovery. The goal is building confidence and capability, not eliminating all risks from your family's digital life.

The Windows XP computer still running in 2015 (and getting attacked daily)

The Donovan family kept their old Windows XP computer running in the home office long after Microsoft stopped supporting it. The machine worked fine for basic tasks like checking email and browsing the web, so they saw no reason to spend money on a replacement. "If it ain't broke, don't fix it," became their technology motto.

What they didn't realize was that their "perfectly good" computer was getting attacked dozens of times per day. Security researchers had discovered hundreds of vulnerabilities in Windows XP after Microsoft stopped releasing patches. Criminals had automated tools that scanned the internet for unprotected XP machines and infected them within minutes of being connected online.

The old computer had become a zombie in a criminal botnet, sending spam emails and attacking other computers without the family's knowledge. Their internet service provider finally shut down their connection after receiving complaints about malicious activity originating from their network.

When I examined the computer, I found 23 different pieces of malware, three cryptocurrency mining programs, and evidence that criminals had been using their machine to store and distribute illegal content. The computer that "worked fine" had been working harder for criminals than for the Donovan family.

The incident taught me that in cybersecurity, standing still is moving backward. Technology that was secure yesterday becomes vulnerable today as criminals develop new attack methods and software vendors stop providing security updates.

Your family's digital security isn't a one-time setup that you can ignore once it's working. It's an ongoing process that requires regular attention, periodic updates, and continuous adaptation to emerging threats.

Regular Security Maintenance Tasks: Your Digital Hygiene Routine

Effective family cybersecurity requires establishing maintenance routines that keep your protection systems current and effective. Just like physical maintenance for your home and car, digital maintenance prevents small problems from becoming expensive disasters.

Monthly Security Checkups

Review all family devices on the first weekend of each month to ensure security software is current, updates are installed, and unusual activity hasn't occurred. Set a recurring calendar reminder so this task doesn't get forgotten during busy periods.

Check password manager reports for weak, reused, or compromised passwords that need attention. Most password managers provide security scores and recommendations for improving your password hygiene.

Monitor credit reports and financial account statements for unauthorized activity that might indicate identity theft or account compromise. Early detection prevents small fraudulent charges from becoming major financial disasters.

Update backup systems and verify that automatic backups are working correctly. Test file restoration from backups periodically to ensure your recovery systems work when you need them.

Review family members' device usage reports and screen time statistics to identify unusual patterns that might indicate compromised accounts or inappropriate access.

Quarterly Deep Maintenance

Perform comprehensive security scans on all family devices using updated security software and malware removal tools. These deep scans catch infections that might have evaded real-time protection.

Review and update privacy settings on social media accounts, cloud storage services, and other online platforms. Companies frequently change privacy policies and add new data collection features that are enabled by default.

Audit user accounts and access permissions for all family online services. Remove old accounts that are no longer needed and revoke access for services and applications that your family no longer uses.

Clean up device storage by removing unnecessary files, old downloads, and cached data that can slow performance and create security risks. Full hard drives often indicate malware infections or compromised systems.

Update emergency contact information and recovery methods for all important accounts. Phone numbers, backup email addresses, and security questions should be current and accessible.

Annual Security Overhaul

Change passwords for all critical accounts even if they haven't been compromised. Annual password rotation reduces the impact of data breaches that might not be discovered or reported immediately.

Review and update your family's incident response plan based on new threats, changed family circumstances, and lessons learned from security incidents during the previous year.

Evaluate your backup and recovery systems to ensure they're adequate for your family's current data storage needs and protection requirements. Storage needs grow faster than most people expect.

Assess insurance coverage for cyber incidents, identity theft, and digital asset protection. Many homeowner's and renter's insurance policies now include cyber coverage that might be relevant for your family.

Research new security tools and services that might provide better protection or easier management than your current solutions. Security technology improves rapidly, and annual reviews help you take advantage of new capabilities.

A family created a shared calendar with specific security tasks assigned to different family members each month. Dad handled password audits, mom managed backup testing, and teenagers were responsible for social media privacy reviews.

Each family member had a checklist of their monthly tasks with specific steps and success criteria. They held brief family meetings to discuss any problems discovered during maintenance and to update procedures based on new threats or changed circumstances.

The distributed approach ensured that security maintenance happened consistently and that multiple family members understood their protection systems. When security incidents occurred, everyone knew their role in response and recovery.

The family's systematic approach took about two hours per month total, but it prevented several potential disasters and gave everyone confidence in their digital protection.

Staying Current with Security Updates

Enable automatic updates for operating systems, security software, and critical applications on all family devices. Manual update management is too burdensome for most families and creates gaps when updates are delayed or forgotten.

Configure devices to install security updates immediately but defer feature updates until you can test them for compatibility problems. Security patches should never be delayed, but major system changes can sometimes create new problems.

Monitor vendor security advisories for devices and software that don't update automatically. Smart home devices, routers, and older computers often require manual update management.

> ★ **Pro Tip:** Create a simple spreadsheet tracking the last update date for each family device and service. This record helps you identify devices that might have missed updates or that need manual attention.

Subscribe to security newsletters and threat intelligence feeds that provide early warning about new attacks targeting home users. Knowledge of emerging threats helps you adjust your protection before attacks become widespread.

Test critical systems after major updates to ensure that security patches haven't broken important functionality. Updates occasionally cause compatibility problems that need immediate attention.

Staying Informed About New Threats

The cybersecurity threat landscape changes constantly as criminals develop new attack methods and security researchers discover new vulnerabilities. Staying informed helps you adapt your protection to address emerging risks.

Reliable Information Sources

Follow reputable cybersecurity organizations and government agencies that provide accurate threat information without sensationalism or marketing bias. The US Cybersecurity and Infrastructure Security Agency (CISA), SANS Institute, and major security vendors provide reliable threat intelligence.

Subscribe to security newsletters from trusted sources that explain new threats in language that non-technical family members can understand. Avoid sources that use fear tactics to sell security products or services.

Join online communities and forums where security professionals discuss emerging threats and protection strategies. Reddit's cybersecurity communities and professional security forums provide valuable insights from experienced practitioners.

Follow security researchers and journalists who specialize in covering threats that affect home users. Many researchers share threat intelligence on social media platforms and professional blogs.

Monitor news sources that cover cybersecurity incidents affecting other families and organizations similar to yours. Learning from other people's security failures helps you avoid similar problems.

Filtering Information Overload

Focus on threats that affect technologies and services your family uses rather than trying to track every possible security risk. Generic threat intelligence often isn't relevant to your specific situation.

Prioritize information about threats that target your family's demographics, geographic location, or technology preferences. Criminals often focus their attacks on specific populations or regions.

Distinguish between theoretical security research and active threats that criminals are exploiting against real targets. Academic security research doesn't always translate to practical risks for home users.

Verify threat information from multiple sources before making significant changes to your security practices. False alarms and exaggerated threats can waste time and resources without providing real protection benefits.

Balance threat awareness with practical security management. Constantly worrying about every possible threat can lead to security fatigue and poor decision-making.

Adapting to New Threats

Evaluate new threats against your family's current protection to determine whether additional security measures are needed. Not every new threat requires immediate action if your existing protections are adequate.

Test new security tools and techniques in non-critical environments before implementing them for your entire family. New protection measures sometimes create usability problems that outweigh their security benefits.

Share threat information with other family members and explain how new risks might affect their daily technology use.

Security education should be ongoing rather than limited to formal training sessions.

Document changes you make to your security practices in response to new threats. This record helps you evaluate the effectiveness of your adaptations and avoid conflicting security measures.

Participate in community security awareness efforts to help protect your neighbors and local organizations from emerging threats. Community-wide security improvements benefit everyone in your area.

> ▲ **Caution:** Don't let fear of new threats drive you to implement security measures that make technology unusable for your family. The goal is reasonable protection, not perfect security that prevents beneficial technology use.

When and How to Upgrade Devices

Technology devices have limited security lifespans because manufacturers eventually stop providing security updates and criminals develop new attack methods that target older systems.

Security-Driven Replacement Timing

Replace devices when manufacturers stop providing security updates, even if the hardware still functions adequately for your family's needs. Unsupported devices become increasingly vulnerable as security researchers discover new vulnerabilities.

Monitor vendor support lifecycles when purchasing new devices to understand how long you can expect to receive security updates. Choose devices with longer support commitments when possible.

Consider replacing devices early when security vulnerabilities are discovered that manufacturers can't or won't fix. Some hardware vulnerabilities require device replacement rather than software updates.

Upgrade devices that can't support current security software or encryption standards. Older devices might work for basic tasks but lack the capabilities needed for modern security protection.

Replace devices that have been compromised by sophisticated malware that might persist despite cleaning efforts. Complete device replacement provides higher confidence in security restoration than attempting to clean compromised systems.

Balancing Security and Economics

Evaluate the cost of security risks against the cost of device replacement when making upgrade decisions. A $300 laptop replacement might be justified to avoid the potential costs of identity theft or data loss.

Consider the total cost of ownership when evaluating device upgrades. Older devices often require more maintenance, support, and security attention that adds to their hidden costs.

Plan device replacement schedules that spread costs over time rather than requiring simultaneous replacement of multiple devices. Gradual replacement is more affordable and allows you to test new devices before committing your entire family to new technology.

Research refurbished and budget devices that provide current security capabilities at lower costs than premium models. Security protection doesn't always require expensive hardware.

Factor security update lifecycles into purchase decisions to maximize the useful life of new devices. Spending slightly more for devices with longer support commitments often provides better long-term value.

Managing Device Transitions

Plan device transitions to minimize disruption to your family's daily activities while ensuring that security protections remain continuous during replacement periods.

Back up all data from old devices before beginning transitions and verify that backups are complete and accessible. Device transitions often reveal backup problems that need immediate attention.

Transfer security software licenses and account access to new devices before disposing of old devices. Some security software limits the number of devices that can use single licenses.

Migrate user accounts, settings, and security configurations to new devices systematically to avoid creating security gaps during transitions. Document the migration process to ensure consistency across multiple device replacements.

Dispose of old devices securely by wiping data completely and physically destroying storage media that contained sensitive information. Standard deletion doesn't remove data securely enough to prevent recovery by determined criminals.

> ■ **Danger Zone:** Never delay security updates or device replacement due to cost concerns. The expense of device replacement is always less than the cost of recovering from major security incidents that could have been prevented.

Planning for the Future of Home Technology

Home technology evolves rapidly, and security planning must account for new devices, services, and threat vectors that will emerge in the coming years.

Emerging Technology Risks

Artificial intelligence integration in home devices creates new privacy and security risks as voice assistants, smart cameras, and other devices gain more sophisticated capabilities for monitoring and analyzing family activities.

Internet of Things expansion continues to add network-connected capabilities to traditional appliances and home systems, creating new attack vectors that require ongoing security attention.

Quantum computing development threatens current encryption standards and will eventually require new security technologies to protect sensitive information from quantum-capable attackers.

Biometric authentication proliferation creates new privacy risks as more devices collect and store fingerprints, facial recognition data, and other biological information.

Cloud service consolidation increases the impact of security breaches as fewer companies control larger portions of families' digital infrastructure and personal data.

Building Adaptable Security

Design security systems that can accommodate new devices and technologies without requiring complete reconstruction of your family's protection infrastructure.

Choose security tools and services that demonstrate commitment to ongoing development and adaptation to emerging threats rather than static solutions that might become obsolete quickly.

Maintain flexibility in your security approach by avoiding dependencies on specific vendors or technologies that might not remain viable long-term.

Invest in security education and skills development that will remain relevant as technology changes rather than focusing only on tool-specific training that might become outdated.

Build relationships with security professionals and community resources that can provide guidance as new threats and technologies emerge.

Creating Sustainable Security Practices

Establish security habits and processes that your family can maintain consistently regardless of specific technologies or threats. Good security principles remain relevant even as tools and risks evolve.

Focus on security fundamentals that apply across different technologies: strong authentication, regular backups, software updates, and careful information sharing practices.

Teach family members to think critically about new technologies and their security implications rather than blindly adopting every new device or service that becomes available.

Plan security budgets that account for ongoing costs of device replacement, software licensing, and professional services rather than treating security as a one-time expense.

Document your security decision-making processes and criteria so that future security choices remain consistent with your family's values and risk tolerance.

Your family's digital security requires ongoing attention, continuous learning, and periodic adaptation to new threats and technologies. The effort you invest in systematic security maintenance pays dividends by preventing disasters and ensuring that your protection remains effective as your family's technology use evolves.

The goal isn't perfect security, which is impossible and impractical for most families. The goal is sustainable security that provides reasonable protection without becoming a burden that prevents your family from benefiting from beneficial technologies.

Remember that security maintenance is a marathon, not a sprint. Consistent attention to security hygiene and gradual improvement of your protection systems provides better long-term security than sporadic efforts to implement perfect solutions.

Conclusion

You've made it through 14 chapters of cybersecurity guidance, and more practical security guidance than you probably thought existed. If you're feeling slightly overwhelmed, that's normal. If you're wondering how families managed to survive the internet for this long without getting completely destroyed by criminals, that's also normal.

Here's the truth: most families survive on luck and the fact that criminals haven't targeted them yet. Your family's digital security has probably been about as systematic as your approach to car maintenance. You know it's important, you mean to deal with it eventually, and you hope nothing breaks before you get around to it.

But cybersecurity affects your family's safety, privacy, and financial security every single day. The criminals targeting families aren't the stereotypical basement dwellers from movies. They're organized professionals who understand family psychology better than most family therapists. They know you're busy, distracted, and trying to balance security with convenience. They design their attacks around these realities.

What You've Accomplished

By reading this book, you've done something most families never do: you've educated yourself about threats that most people ignore until they become victims. You now understand why your neighbor's smart TV was sending spam emails, why your friend's social media account started posting cryptocurrency scams, and why your elderly relative keeps getting phone calls from "Microsoft technical support."

You know the difference between security theater that makes you feel protected and security measures that provide real protection. You understand why complex passwords that humans can't remember are often less secure than simple passwords that families can use consistently. You've learned that the most expensive security software in the world won't protect a family that clicks on everything that looks interesting.

Most importantly, you've learned to think like the criminals who target families. You understand their business model, their preferred attack methods, and the psychological tricks they use to bypass technical security measures. This knowledge provides protection that adapts to new threats even when specific tools and techniques become outdated.

The Reality of Family Cybersecurity

Perfect security is impossible for families because perfect security would prevent you from doing anything useful with technology. The goal isn't eliminating all risks. It's reducing your family's risk profile to levels that let you sleep peacefully while still benefiting from the digital tools that make modern life convenient and connected.

Your family's security will never be finished. It's an ongoing process that evolves as your family grows, as technology changes, and as criminals develop new attack methods. The security measures that protect your elementary school children won't work for teenagers who need more independence. The simple backup system that works today might not be adequate when your family's digital life expands beyond what fits on a single computer.

This ongoing evolution isn't a burden. It's an opportunity to build security habits that grow stronger as your family gains experience. Families who start with basic protection and gradually improve their security develop better long-term protection than families who try to implement perfect security immediately and abandon it when it becomes too difficult to maintain.

Your Next Steps

Don't try to implement everything in this book simultaneously. Choose three security improvements that address your family's biggest current risks and implement them well before moving on to additional measures. A simple password manager that your family uses consistently provides better protection than a sophisticated security system that gets abandoned after two weeks.

Start with the fundamentals that protect against the most common threats: secure your home network, implement basic device security, and establish family policies about sharing personal information online. These foundations protect against 80% of the attacks that target families while providing a platform for more advanced security measures as your family's technical skills develop.

Test your security measures periodically to ensure they're working as expected and that all family members understand how to use them during emergencies. Security that only works when everything goes perfectly isn't security at all. It's wishful thinking dressed up with expensive software.

Building Security Culture in Your Family

The most secure families aren't those with the most advanced technology. They're families where security awareness becomes part of the family culture. Children who grow up understanding why passwords matter and how criminals operate develop intuitive security habits that protect them throughout their lives.

Make security discussions a regular part of family life, not crisis responses to problems that have occurred. Celebrate when family members identify potential threats or follow good security practices. Create an environment where admitting security mistakes leads to problem-solving instead of punishment.

Remember that your family's security is only as strong as its least technical member. The time you invest in helping elderly relatives, young children, and less technical family members understand and implement basic security measures protects your entire family's digital environment.

The Future of Family Digital Security

Technology will continue evolving faster than most families can adapt, and criminals will continue developing new ways to exploit emerging technologies. Artificial intelligence will create new opportunities for both protection and attack. Smart home devices will continue proliferating faster than security standards can be established. New social media platforms will emerge with privacy policies that most families won't read or understand.

But the fundamental principles of family cybersecurity remain constant: strong authentication, regular updates, careful information sharing, reliable backups, and educated decision-making. Families who master these fundamentals can adapt to new technologies and threats more successfully than families who focus only on specific tools that might become obsolete.

The goal isn't becoming cybersecurity experts. It's developing enough knowledge and good habits to make your family an unattractive target for criminals who prefer easier victims. In the cybersecurity world, you don't need to outrun the bear; you just need to outrun the other families who haven't invested any effort in protection.

Final Thoughts

Your family deserves to benefit from digital technology without becoming victims of digital crime. The convenience, connection, and opportunities that technology provides shouldn't come at the cost of your privacy, safety, or peace of mind.

The security measures in this book aren't theoretical recommendations from someone who's never implemented them in real family environments. They're practical solutions developed through decades of helping families recover from cyber incidents and tested in households with children, seniors, and family members spanning the full range of technical comfort levels.

You now have the knowledge to protect your family's digital life. The question isn't whether you can implement effective security. It's whether you will. Your family's protection depends on the actions you take, not the intentions you have.

Start today. Start small. Start with what matters most to your family's specific situation. But start.

Your family's digital future depends on the security foundation you build now.

About the Author

Richard Lowe brings 45 years of technology leadership and cybersecurity expertise to family digital protection. As Director of Computer Operations at Trader Joe's for nearly two decades, he managed IT infrastructure supporting a $16 billion retail operation with 474+ stores and 38,000+ employees, overseeing critical systems from warehouse management to point-of-sale operations and comprehensive cybersecurity including annual PCI DSS compliance.

His technology foundation began when computing required genuine expertise: managing PDP-11 systems, hand-coding in assembly language, and building everything from complete accounting systems to pioneering disk defragmentation software. At Software Techniques, Beck Computer Systems, and BIF Accutel, he led teams developing breakthrough fraud detection systems and managing SCADA implementations for major water utilities, establishing the behavioral analytics foundation that evolved into modern AI-driven security systems.

Richard's cybersecurity credentials include official recognition as Technical Editor for KnowBe4's published book "Cyberheist," multiple CERT-LA emergency response certifications, and real-world disaster survival experience: three 7.1+ magnitude earthquakes and four hurricanes. His practical security expertise earned academic validation when Professor Richard Makadok at Purdue University's Krannert School of Management adopted Richard's consulting book as required reading and regularly invites him as a guest speaker.

As author of 113+ books across cybersecurity, business, and emergency preparedness, Richard translates complex technical concepts into practical guidance that non-technical families can implement successfully. His bestselling "Focus on LinkedIn" sold 15,000 copies in three days, and his works have been professionally translated into seven languages, demonstrating global recognition of his ability to make technology accessible.

Richard's combination of Fortune 500 technology leadership, published cybersecurity expertise, emergency response certification, and family-focused communication skills provides the rare blend of technical authority and practical accessibility that families need to protect their digital lives without becoming cybersecurity experts themselves.

Professional validation includes endorsements from certified cybersecurity professionals, media appearances on 55+ podcasts including The Chris Voss Show (1M+ listeners), and measurable client outcomes spanning decades of helping families and businesses implement effective digital protection strategies that work in real-world environments.

Books by Richard Lowe

See books by Richard Lowe at
https://masterofworlds.com

Get free publishing insights and industry updates at
https://thewritingking.substack.com

For ghostwriting and book coaching services see
https://thewritingking.com

www.ingramcontent.com/pod-product-compliance
Lightning Source LLC
Chambersburg PA
CBHW032015050726
47590CB00006B/2189